Portrait of a Decade

The 1920s

BETTY WILLIAMS

B.T. Batsford Ltd, London

Contents

© Betty Williams 1989
First published 1989

Typeset by Tek-Art Ltd Kent
and printed and bound
in Great Britain by
The Bath Press, Bath
for the publishers
B.T. Batsford Ltd
4 Fitzhardinge Street
London W1H 0AH

ISBN 0 7134 5816 X

*Frontispiece: practising the Charleston. The
dance arrived in Britain in 1925.*

Introduction

The 1920s started with high hopes and high ideals. It seemed to many, in the age which has been called The Roaring Twenties, that at last the world was going to turn over a new leaf, to make a change for the better.

The Great War, the 'war to end wars', was over and in Britain soldiers returning from the terrible carnage of the trenches were promised 'a land fit for heroes to live in'. The League of Nations, formed by the victorious powers, heralded an era of peace and co-operation between the countries of the world.

New discoveries in science, new developments in technology, made almost anything seem possible. It was the age of the pioneer. In the same year – 1919 – that Alcock and Brown made the first flight across the Atlantic, regular passenger air-services started between London and Europe. Soon flimsy-looking planes were covering the world in a series of 'hops' from continent to continent. Flying was taken up as a sport and air-circuses demonstrated daring feats of loop-the-loop to amazed onlookers.

On land, racing motorists pushed their cars towards the 200 mph barrier, which Britain's Henry Seagrave broke in 1927. For the first time, too, people of more modest means were able to become motorists. Manufacturers like Henry Ford in America and Morris and Austin in Britain mass-produced cars which were reasonably-priced and easy to drive.

For the many who could not afford a car, new opportunities were nevertheless opened up by the development of motor transport. Now they could climb into a charabanc for the works outing to the seaside or go by motor-bus on the Sunday School treat.

In Edwardian times women had worn their best flounced dresses and picture hats to look beautiful in the back of an 'open tourer'. Now they took to the wheel themselves. From Cincinnati to Croydon and even in Constantinople women were more emancipated than they had ever been. Fashion reflected the freer spirit. By mid-decade short skirts and short hair were the norm in Europe and America. In London's West End the Bright Young Things kicked up their heels – literally – against the fusty conventions of their Edwardian forebears. Chirpy songs like 'Yes, we have no bananas!' swept the world and flappers girated with 'syncopation' to the new rhythms of jazz.

It was an age of innovation in art and literature too. Writers like James Joyce and Virginia Woolf broke through the barriers of convention to produce works in a new 'stream of consciousness' form. In art this was matched by *Surrealism*, which tried to reach a new reality by interpreting the workings of the sub-conscious mind. In design, *Art Deco* underlined the spirit of the age with an angular, no-nonsense look.

A new window was opened on the world for millions of people by the cinema. Once or twice a week they were able to forget their humdrum lives in the plush surroundings of the local Picture Palace. There they could swoon over romantic Hollywood stars such as Rudolph Valentino or Mary Pickford, laugh at the comic antics of Charlie Chaplin or follow the cartoon adventures of Felix the Cat and Mickey Mouse.

In their own homes, too, there was an exciting new medium of entertainment and information. The 1920s was the first decade of public broadcasting. From 1922 when the BBC was formed, the popularity of the wireless grew and grew. In the first year, 125,000 people bought 10s licences

This 1920s advertisement shows a wireless powered by valves.

Introduction

to 'listen in' but by 1930 the number had risen to over 3 million. From 1924 the first experiments were being made in television.

Great strides were made in other fields of science and technology, especially medicine. Discoveries like that of insulin and penicillin meant that the lives of many sufferers suddenly held new hope. In the realm of public health, too, immunization against diseases vastly improved conditions, especially among poorer people. Birth control clinics were pioneered.

But there was a darker side to the twenties. As early as 1921 economic depression and unemployment were casting their shadows across the page. Ex-servicemen, jobless and living in slum houses, found the promise of a better land had been merely an election slogan. After 1921 there was never less than one million unemployed in Britain and life 'on the dole' in the North of England or South Wales was very different to that of the Bright Young Things in Mayfair.

Britain's first Labour government took office in 1924 but with a minority in the House of Commons lasted less than a year. Subsequent wage cuts for the miners led to the country's first and only general strike in 1926.

New political philosophies emerged in Europe to challenge the beliefs held by the democratic governments, which were beginning to flounder among the rocks of economic recession. In Italy Mussolini, the first of the Fascist dictators, made his famous March on Rome in 1922. After a military coup the following year, Primo de Rivera set up a Fascist government in Spain. Hitler attempted a Nazi take-over in Germany in 1923 but did not in fact come to power until the 1930s. He published *Mein Kampf* in 1925 and in the latter years of the decade his brown-shirted thugs, like Mussolini's blackshirts, carried out vicious campaigns against those who opposed them.

Communism in Russia took on an equally hard face after the death of Lenin in 1924. When Stalin assumed power the stage was set for a clamp-down on individuality and for searing purges of all political dissidents.

Throughout the decade China was wracked by civil war. Though Mustapha Kemal started a programme of modernization in Turkey, problems were building up in other parts of the Middle East where religious differences were to be the spur for years of conflict.

Despite a mamoth Empire Exhibition at Wembley, the days of the old British Empire were numbered, and Commonwealth countries were given equal status with Britain during the decade. In India Gandhi led a campaign of civil disobedience against British rule. The 'Irish problem' was ended with a settlement between Britain and a new Free State in 1922 but Northern Ireland remained as part of the United Kingdom. In-built in the compromise were the causes of further 'troubles' to come.

The idealism embodied in the League of Nations Convention did result in some real achievements in international relations. Notable were the Locarno treaties settling European boundaries in 1925 and the Kellogg-Briand Pact of 1928. But this pact in which 65 nations renounced war, was like the League itself in that high ideals were not backed by any coercive powers. In the tougher climate of the 1930s the League was to prove powerless to deal with strong-armed totalitarian aggressors.

The United States did not join the League. Isolationism seemed an attractive policy to many Americans who wanted to turn their backs on the

Ex-soldiers, dubbed the Black and Tans, were recruited in England to aid the Irish police.

Inside one of Marie Stopes's birth control clinics in the 1920s.

4

Introduction

tangled problems of Europe. Even so, in the 1920s the American way of life had more influence on the rest of the world and especially on Britain and Europe than ever before. Films and fashion, drinks and dances, jazz and jalopies crossed the Atlantic to a public avidly waiting to receive them, but in 1929 it was an event in America which ended the good times with a loud bang.

The Wall Street Crash truly marked the end of an era. It was an era which in many ways was flamboyant and uncaring and, as totalitarian tyrannies built up in Europe, one that was shot through with menace. But it was also distinguished by an exciting spirit of youth and adventure. The feeling that anything might be achieved – even peace and prosperity – was ended by the economic depression which followed the Crash. The high jinks of the Bright Young Things gave way to brittle bravado and for many millions life became a sullen struggle to exist.

As the decade came to a close people asked themselves: how had so many opportunities slipped from their grasp? Had the Roaring Twenties, the Jazz Age, the age which had seemed poised at the start of a new and better world, been just an age of illusion after all?

Henry Seagrave stands beside the Golden Arrow, *the car in which he broke the land speed record in 1929.*

Prohibition

ON 16 JANUARY AMERICA WENT 'DRY'. All alcoholic drinks were banned under an Act amending the Constitution. The era of Prohibition, as it was called, lasted throughout the 1920s. Prohibition followed years of campaigning by anti-drink societies such as the Anti-Saloon League and the Women's Christian Temperance Union, which believed alcohol to be ungodly, evil and wasteful. Several states had passed prohibition laws in the nineteenth century and a National Prohibition party contested the Presidential election in 1892. Prohibition was promoted by Protestants on both religious and economic grounds. Grain, used in brewing, was needed for food during the First World War so in 1917 its use in the manufacture of alcohol was banned. Prohibition received a boost at this time because of hostility to Germany. Many German immigrants to America worked in the brewing industry and beer-drinking was regarded as a Germanic trait. *The American Issue*, an anti-alcohol paper whose slogan was: 'A Saloonless Nation and a Stainless Flag', declared on 17 January:

All Liquor Stains Wiped From the Stars and Stripes . . . . Faith and devotion have triumphed. The American saloon with its long train of attendant evils has been overthrown . . . . No more will broken-hearted, poverty-stricken mothers be seen in very agony of soul, wringing their hands at the graves of drunken sons . . . Christmas will be an occasion of joy and cheer in the home – no longer one of dire apprehension of a drunken husband and father's home-coming. Daddy, too, will be more indus-trious, a better provider . . . . The state will have less crime to prosecute . . . . There will be an increase in respect for law . . . .

Crime and corruption

THE AMERICAN ISSUE WAS WRONG. Drunkenness *had* been widespread before the ban, but prohibition in fact marked the start of a decade of unprecedented crime, corruption – and drinking. Immediately the Act became law, a huge operation for the illegal manufacture and sale of alcohol started up.

Bootlegging

ILLICIT SPIRITS known as 'bootleg liquor' were made in hidden stills. Alcohol was hijacked from consignments of medical supplies, and smuggled in by sea from the West Indies or overland through Canada. Illegal brewing became big business, though some of the drinks, described as 'wood alcohol', could make people very ill and were reputed to cause blindness.

Straw-hatted Americans drink behind closed doors in a speak-easy bar.

Speak-easies

AT HOME IT WAS SMART to have a bar hidden behind the bookcase – 'I was T.T. until prohibition', joked the comedian Groucho Marx. On the streets speak-easies, disguised as soft-drinks saloons, opened on every corner to sell illicit liquor to anyone who could say the right password. They had an aura of glamour and excitement.

I loved speak-easies. If you knew the right ones you never worried about being poisoned by bad whiskey. The speaks were so romantic. A pretty girl in a speak-easy was the most beautiful girl in the world. As soon as you walked in the door you were a special person, you belonged to a special society. When I'd bring a person in, it was like dispensing largesse. I was a big man. You had to know somebody who knew somebody. It had that marvellous movie-like quality, unreality . . . . I started drinking in speaks. I didn't know about open drinking, to go off in the street and order a drink without having an arm on your shoulder. I'd gotten used to the idea of being disreputable. Alec Wilder, New York composer, quoted in *Hard Times* by Studs Terkel.

'dry'

Gang warfare

CHICAGO – 'the wickedest city in the world' – was the centre of the illicit liquor business. This was controlled by gangsters but Chicago's police force, town hall officials, politicians and even judges were involved in the 'racket'. Gang-leader Johnny Torrio boasted: 'I own the police.' 'Protection money' was paid to the gangs by the owners of speak-easies, night clubs and gambling dens. The police were bribed not to raid protected places. Those who did not pay got a visit from an 'education committee' which smashed up the premises.

Warfare between rival gangs reached horrific proportions. There were at least 500 gang killings in Chicago during Prohibition. The first major murder was in May, less than four months after the start of the drinks ban. Vice-king 'Diamond Jim' Colosimo went to a 'business appointment' and was killed by unknown assassins.

Al Capone

TORRIO TOOK OVER Colosimo's 'empire', assisted by the man who was to become known as 'Public Enemy No.1': Al Capone. Italian-born 'Scarface' Capone arrived in Chicago from New York early in 1920 to help Torrio 'take care of the competition'. He soon succeeded his boss as 'King' of Chicago's gangland and was head of a multi-million dollar drinks and vice syndicate. Flashily dressed and smoking a big cigar, he was driven around Chicago in a bullet-proof Cadillac with a machine-gunner sitting in the front seat.

Eighteenth amendment

. . . . THE MANUFACTURE, sale or transportation of intoxicating liquors within, the importation thereof into, or the exportation thereof from the United States and all territory subject to the jurisdiction thereof for beverage purposes is hereby prohibited.

Al Capone in the 1920s – a smart dresser as well as a 'smart operator'.

Peace moves – League's first session

AFTER THE HORRORS of the First World War, everyone's hope was that it had been 'the war to end wars'. It was felt that only by nations working together to settle disputes harmoniously could peace be preserved. This belief led to the formation of the League of Nations, which held its first session in Paris in January.

Forty-one countries were represented but several important ones were missing. Russia was excluded; Germany and other 'ex-enemy' states were not allowed to belong. Though US President Woodrow Wilson had been the dominant force behind the setting up of the League, America was overcome by a wave of isolationism. Rejecting his ideals, other politicians decided to turn their backs on the problems of Europe: America did not join the League. Britain and France thus became the leading members in the early days of the new peace-keeping institution.

The League, which soon moved to a new headquarters in Geneva, had a General Assembly and a smaller Council with five permanent and several temporary member-nations. A Permanent Court of International Justice was set up at the Hague in Holland, and an International Labour Organization aimed at improving working conditions throughout the world.

The League, however, was rather like a guard dog without teeth. It had no international armed force to back up its decisions in disputes between nations. Instead, members agreed to use economic sanctions against countries which threatened armed attacks or resorted to war.

THE HIGH CONTRACTING PARTIES
In order to promote international co-operation and to achieve international peace and security
    by the acceptance of obligations not to resort to war,
    by the prescription of open, just and honourable relations between nations,
    by the firm establishment of the under-standing of international law as the actual rule of conduct among Governments, and
    by the maintenance of justice and a scrupulous respect for all treaty obligations in the dealings of organized peoples with one another,
    Agree to this Covenant of the League of Nations.
From the Covenant of the League of Nations

Armistice Day

THE BODY OF AN UNKNOWN SOLDIER who died in battle was buried in Westminster Abbey on 11 November, a symbolic grave for all those who were killed in the war. King George V unveiled Britain's national memorial – the Cenotaph – in Whitehall. Towns and villages throughout the land put up memorials to commemorate their own dead.

A village war memorial in Surrey.

Unemployment benefits extended

BY THE BEGINNING OF THE YEAR millions of men demobilized from the armed forces were looking for jobs. Though industry had boomed in Britain just after the war, a slump was starting in 1920 and unemployment began to rise. David Lloyd George, the Liberal Prime Minister of the Coalition government, brought in a new Unemployment Insurance Act to replace the one of 1911, which had limited the 'dole' to workers in three industries. Now 15s a week was paid to most men, and 12s a week to women, who were out of a job. Those in work paid weekly insurance contributions to help finance the scheme and so did their employers. During the 1920s the average wage of a skilled worker was between £3 and £5 a week.

Black and Tans for Ireland

IN IRELAND a newly created Irish Republican Army waged a campaign of guerilla warfare against the British who, despite a promise to work towards Irish 'Home Rule', were still struggling to govern the country. The political party Sinn Fein ('Ourselves Alone') defied the British government by setting up its own parliament, the Dail, in Dublin. IRA 'flying columns' scoured the country, burning police barracks, ambushing British soldiers and shooting British sympathizers.

Few Irishmen would now join the Royal Irish Constabulary, Ireland's police force, so two groups of men were hastily recruited in Britain to go to its aid. The first group, mainly unemployed ex-servicemen, signed on for a wage of 10s a day and 'all found'. They wore an improvised uniform of blackish-green caps and tunics with khaki trousers. The Irish quickly dubbed them the 'Black and Tans' after the hounds of a famous Limerick foxhunt. They were joined by the Auxiliaries, who were all ex-Army officers from the 1914-18 war. Between them they waged their own campaign of terrorism against the Irish population.

Black and Tans search a suspected IRA man in Ireland.

Burnt cork incident

SOME OF THE WORST INCIDENTS in this tit-for-tat war took place in and around Cork, a Republican stronghold in the south-west where one of the most ruthless of the IRA leaders, Tom Barry, headed a 'flying column'.

In November 16 'Auxies' were killed in an IRA ambush. Cork was put under military rule but the next day there was another ambush. In revenge, Black and Tans raided the city in an orgy of wrecking and looting. Much of the city centre was destroyed by fire and afterwards the 'Tans' paraded the streets wearing burnt corks in their caps.

This incident shocked public opinion in Britian and helped to swing the mood of the country against the government's policy of answering force with force, and in favour of negotiating a settlement of the 'Irish question'.

Polish push

POLAND, which became an independent state after the war, attacked Russia in April and captured Kiev. The Red Army finally drove the Polish forces back and a treaty settling national boundaries was signed in October. This year marked the end of opposition to the new Communist state, which had suffered three years of civil war against 'White Russian' forces. Lenin, the Soviet leader, was now free to start the reconstruction of his country.

Feminine Franchise

AFTER A LONG AND BITTER CAMPAIGN, American women were given the vote on equal terms with men. In Britain women over 30 were enfranchised in 1919 but those under 30 had to wait until 1928 to get the vote.

Chaplin makes *The Kid*

CHARLIE CHAPLIN, 'THE LITTLE FELLOW' who was the comic genius of the silent screen, made his first full length film, *The Kid*, in 1920. He was one of a number of stars whom people flocked to see at their local Picture Palace or Kinema. Others included Mary Pickford – 'the world's sweetheart' – Douglas Fairbanks, a swashbuckling hero of screen drama, Pearl White, Tom Mix and the romantic Rudolph Valentino. Though the films were silent, captions were put on the screen and most cinemas had an accompanist who played appropriate music on a cinema organ or piano – fast and furious during a cowboy chase, slow and dreamy during a love scene. By the mid-twenties millions of people in Britain went to the cinema every week. Numerous magazines related the news of the Hollywood scene to them.

Novel shocks small town America

MAIN STREET, A NOVEL published by American writer Sinclair Lewis in 1920, shocked the stolid citizens of the Mid-West with its depiction of the smug conformity of small-town life as seen through the eyes of a go-ahead city girl.

She had fancied that all the world was changing. She found that it was not. In Gopher Prairie the only ardent new topics were prohibition, the place in Minneapolis where you could get whisky at thirteen dollars a quart, recipies for home-made beer, the 'high cost of living' . . . . Main Street, with its two-storey brick shops, its storey-and-a-half wooden residences, its muddy expanse from concrete walk to walk, its huddle of Fords and lumber-wagons, was too small to absorb her . . . . Oozing out from every drab wall, she felt a forbidding spirit which she could never conquer.
(*Main Street*)

Readers voted these filmstars top in a popularity poll conducted by Picture Show *magazine.*

Thrills at Wimbledon

WILLIAM TILDEN WON the men's singles at Wimbledon in 1920, notching up the first success for the United States in the history of the championships. Tall and flamboyant, 'Big Bill' won again in 1921 and 1930 and was seven times US champion.

The French player, Suzanne Lenglen, won the women's singles at Wimbledon six times between 1919 and 1926. She heralded a new era, not only in tennis style but in fashion too. Gone was the decorous pat-ball game of pre-war women players; gone too the long skirts, formal blouse and tie. Crowds at Wimbledon were thrilled by Lenglen's athletic play, described by one sports reporter as 'an acrobatic art'. Modern young women copied her short skirts and sleeveless tops, and tied their bobbed hair back with bright-coloured bandeaux like she did. The French player's success was matched later in the decade by an American, Helen Wills, who took her first singles title in 1927 and went on to win Wimbledon six times in a row.

First radio broadcasts

THE ITALIAN INVENTOR GUGLIELMO MARCONI succeeded in transmitting a radio signal across the Atlantic in 1901 but it was not until 1920 that broadcasting to the public began. Thousands of commercial wireless stations opened in the United States but at first Marconi's experimental transmissions from his works in Chelmsford, Essex, were the only ones in Britain. They were received by amateur enthusiasts on home-made crystal radios, known as 'cat's whisker' sets because of the fine piece of wire needed to 'tune in'.

Dame Nellie Melba singing into a microphone at the first 'concert by wireless'.

Fabrics with zip

NEW MATERIALS and a modern invention had a big influence on fashion in the 1920s. Artificial silk, later known as rayon, was developed from wood pulp before the war. It was manufactured in large quantities after 1920. It had a dramatic effect on women's stockings. Before, those who could not afford real silk had worn stockings in heavy, dark lisle or wool. Now, lightweight rayon hose in flesh-coloured beige or even bright pink was available on the mass market. 'Art-silk' dresses were popular in the cheaper ranges and a new material with a locknit-stitch appeared in 1920 under the brand name 'Celanese'. It was widely used for underwear.

The zip, invented in Chicago in 1893, arrived in Britain in 1919 as the Ready Fastener and was exhibited in 1924 at the British Empire Exhibition. It was used at first for sports clothes. Fashion designers tried it in the late 20s but it was not risked in men's trousers until the mid-30s. Even then, most men would only trust buttons.

Melba sings

A PUBLIC 'CONCERT BY WIRELESS' sponsored by the *Daily Mail* on 15 June marked the start of public broadcasting in Britain. Dame Nellie Melba, the famous Australian prima donna, sang 'over the ether' (as it was called) and was even received by listeners on ships at sea.

We had the Melba wireless concert last night. She went down to the Marconi place at Chelmsford. We had to arrange for a light supper for her of chicken and champagne. Soon after seven o'clock she started singing into a microphone hooked up with a 15 kw set transmitting on 2,800 metres wavelength. I listened in at Blackfriars – frame aerial and telephones, not enough to go round. We listened in turns. Melba's girl secretary was there. Her eyes nearly came out of her head as she heard the nightingale voice in 'Addio' from *La Boheme*. 'It *is* Melba', she cried in astonishment. I think she had not believed us up to that moment.
Tom Clark, *My Northcliffe Diary*

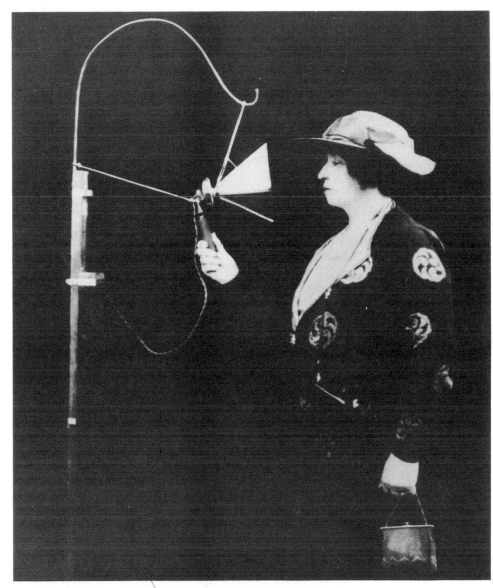

British proposals

NEW PROPOSALS which the British Prime Minister Lloyd George believed would 'shatter the foundation of the ancient hatred and distrust which has disfigured our common history for centuries past' were put forward in a Government of Ireland Act.

Under it, Northern Ireland would remain as part of the United Kingdom while Southern Ireland would become a self-governing Dominion in the British Commonwealth. At first Sinn Fein, led by its president, Eamonn De Valera, held out against any link with Britain. In a letter to Lloyd George, De Valera wrote:

The Irish people's belief is that the national destiny can best be realised in political detachment, free from imperialistic entanglements . . . true friendship with England, which military coercion has frustrated for centuries, can be obtained most readily now through amicable but absolute separation.
Public Record Office: CAB 24/127

As republicans, De Valera and other Sinn Fein leaders objected to Ireland joining the Commonwealth, whose head was the British reigning monarch. At first they held out for a free, united and republican Ireland.

Negotiations lead to treaty

LATER IN THE YEAR, however, worn down by the bitter guerilla warfare – known as 'The Troubles' – the Irish decided to send a delegation to London to discuss an agreement.

It was led by Arthur Griffith, the Sinn Fein founder, and Michael Collins, 'the big fellow' who was the IRA's Director of Intelligence. Against the wishes of De Valera, who opposed the settlement, they signed a treaty on 6 December which embodied the British proposals for a divided Ireland. It was the sort of compromise which, in an attempt to please everybody, satisfied no one. It caused as many problems as it solved. In a mood of desperate foreboding, Collins wrote to a friend that night:

When you have sweated, toiled, had mad dreams, hopeless nightmares, you find

PUNCH, OR THE LONDON CHARIVARI.—November 16, 1921.

A CABINET PICTURE.

MR. LLOYD GEORGE (to Miss Ulster). "A LEETLE TOO SERIOUS, MY DEAR; I WANT TO SEE THAT NICE SMILE OF YOURS. COME, NOW; LOOK AT THE PRETTY DICKY-BIRD."

Cartoon comment in Punch *magazine on Lloyd George's settlement for Northern Ireland.*

King opens Ulster Parliament

THE ULSTER UNIONISTS, who were fiercely Protestant, were as much opposed to the treaty as De Valera. They wanted the whole of Ireland to remain as part of Britain, governed from Westminster. But rather than risk government by Catholics in Dublin, were the Southern Irish Parliament sat, they decided to compromise by accepting limited Home Rule for Ulster with their own Parliament in Belfast.

Despite threats that he might be assassinated, King George V opened the Northern Irish Parliament with a statesmanlike speech appealing for 'an end of strife'. It was written on the advice of the South African war leader, General Jan Smuts. The King appealed:

to all Irishmen to pause, to stretch out the hand of forebearance and conciliation, to forgive and forget and to join in making for the land which they love a new era of peace, contentment and goodwill.
Quoted in F.S.L. Lyons, *Ireland since the Famine*

British soldiers on duty in Dublin during the 'Troubles'.

yourself in London's streets, cold and dank in the night air. Think – what have I got for Ireland? Something which she has wanted these past seven hundred years. Will anyone be satisfied at the bargain? Will anyone? I tell you this – early this morning I signed my death warrant.
Quoted in *Ireland since the Famine*

Agreement

Partition of Ireland

THOUGH THE ANCIENT KINGDOM OF Ulster consisted of nine counties, the new Ulster had only the six which were predominantly Protestant. Irish nationalists in the South, which was largely Catholic, were told by Lloyd George that adjustments could be made to the border later. A Boundary Commission was set up for this purpose.

One of Lloyd George's proposals had been for joint government of North and South. He and other British politicians did not view the partition of the country as necessarily a permanent solution to Ireland's problems. He wrote:

The British Government entertain an earnest hope that the necessity of harmonious co-operation amongst Irishmen of all classes and creeds will be recognized throughout Ireland, and they will welcome the day when by these means unity is achieved. But no such common action can be secured by force . . . .
Public Record Office: CAB 24/126

Home Rule

THE CAMPAIGN FOR IRISH HOME RULE started in the nineteenth century; two of Gladstone's Home Rule bills were defeated in Parliament. The principle was accepted by Britain in 1914 but nothing was done because of the First World War. In the Easter Rising of 1916 Irish nationalists and republicans demanded immediate independence for the whole of Ireland. Protestant Ulster was opposed to this. After the war, in a climate of mounting violence, politicians faced the almost super-human task of thrashing out a settlement acceptable to all sides.

Depression and unemployment

BY NOW INDUSTRIAL DEPRESSION was taking hold all over Europe and in June the number of unemployed in Britain rose to two million, out of a population of 42½ million. The number later dropped, but throughout the decade there were never less than a million out of work. Desperate ex-servicemen rushed for any jobs available. Many of the unlucky ones tried to earn a few 'coppers' selling matches on the street or 'busking' to theatre queues.

An advertisement for a few unskilled handymen drew nearly 2000 unemployed to High Holborn yesterday. Although only six men were required a large crowd of workless men assembled early, and so large did the numbers grow that the police had to organize a queue. The applicants included many skilled men.
Daily Chronicle, 25 August

Unemployed men queueing for the 'dole'.

New housing measures

THE 'LAND FIT FOR HEROES TO LIVE IN', which Lloyd George had promised in the post-war election, was an illusion. A severe housing shortage meant that many people, as well as being out of work, suffered terrible overcrowding in old and dilapidated slum houses where water had to be carried from a communal tap in the yard and an outside lavatory shared with the rest of the street.

A newly-formed Ministry of Health took over the responsibility for housing and paid local authorities a subsidy to help them build houses to let at reasonable rents. The new council housing programme was soon another victim of the depression and by the summer of 1921 grants for building were drastically cut. They were restored to some extent in the mid-twenties.

Pit problems – miners strike

BRITISH COAL MINES were hard hit by the slump in industry. They had been under government control during the war and the miners hoped they would remain so. But in March the pits were handed back to their former owners, who decided that the only way out of their economic troubles was to cut the miners' wages. The miners stopped work but a general strike was averted when railway and transport workers refused to join them in spite of an agreement called the Triple Alliance. In this the unions in the three key industries pledged to support each other in strike action. The failure of their allies to do so caused much resentment among the miners, who were forced eventually to accept lower wages from the coal owners.

Lenin's policy

COMMUNIST HOPES THAT WORKERS in other countries would spontaneously start revolutions of their own on the Russian model faded in the 1920s. Soviet leaders were fully occupied with problems at home.

A mutiny at the Baltic port of Kronstadt, by sailors demanding more democratic rights, was crushed in March. In the same month, however, Lenin brought in a New Economic Policy, which relaxed the strict state controls on the peasants. They were now allowed to sell their surplus crops privately and to pay people to work for them. Peasants with larger farms – the kulaks – began to prosper.

Famine in Russia

THE ECONOMIC SITUATION was still grim in Russia and now part of the country, which had been laid waste by civil war, was in the grip of famine. Drought and harvest failures left millions dying of starvation in a large area of Russia. Long columns of refugees fled the devastated villages in search of help, but millions of peasants perished from hunger and disease. Help was given by international agencies such as the Red Cross.

Writing to his brother in Berlin, a Soviet official, N. Lutovinov, described a journey through the famine-striken areas of the Volga river:

In Samara we found ourselves in the heart of the famine area. There is absolutely nothing there. Three months blazing drought had burnt up everything. There had been no rain, and now the locusts, which had come from the South, are themselves perishing for lack of food . . . . About this time formerly the whole district was in the fields gathering in the harvest, and what have we now?

Blackened fields; abandoned villages, in which only the aged remain to die in their corners . . . . Where are the people gone out of the villages? Men point to the East in the direction of Orenburg Steppes. We met two or three such hordes on our way . . . . You can trace the track of these hordes by the burnt, black lines of the Steppe – bodies of horses, remains of bivouacs, and – sometimes – human bodies . . . .
Public Record Office: CAB 24/127

German payments fixed

REPARATIONS – the amount Germany had to pay to the Allies for loss and damage during the war – were fixed in April at £6.6 billion. A first instalment of £50 million was handed over but, as inflation rose and the economic depression grew worse, it became impossible for Germany to continue payments.

Airship disaster

IN AUGUST, THE BRITISH R38, the biggest airship ever built, took her final test flight before being sold to the USA. British and American crews were on board when the giant flying machine – nearly 700 feet long – split in two and fell in flames into the Humber off Hull. Forty-four people were killed and there were only five survivors.

As she came closer the envelope appeared to crumple in the centre . . . . suddenly she broke clean in two. Up to that time I had seen no flames but all at once there was a terrific explosion, and the falling envelope burst into flames . . . . It is a mercy that the airship got over the river before any explosion took place.
Eye-witness account by Hull pier master.

The R38 leaving her hangar shortly before the disaster.

Sport for all

NOT ONLY WATCHING, but also taking part in sport, was a popular pastime for all sorts of people in the 1920s. Thousands of young men and women, spurred on by the example of the Wimbledon stars, joined tennis clubs or played on municipal courts. More people were able to take day-trips or holidays where they enjoyed a dip in the sea. Many towns opened their own bathing pools. Golf, once restricted to the wealthy, was taken up by middle-class and professional people and new courses were opened outside many major cities. Cycling, hiking and camping were all popular outdoor activities. Team games, such as football and hockey, received encouragement when the National Playing Fields Association was set up to help provide more sports fields for amateurs. School teams, for girls as well as boys, also flourished.

Innovatory art

IN ART, THE 1920S were distinguished by a new creativity and a new urge to experiment. The Spanish painter Pablo Picasso was working in Paris throughout the decade. He was still in his cubist period at the beginning of the twenties and painted a famous cubist work, *The Three Masked Musicians*, in 1921. Also working in Paris at this time were the artists Georges Braque and Fernand Leger, and the architect Le Corbusier, whose approach to building design was startlingly modernistic.

In Germany, too, there was an innovatory spirit. Walter Gropius started a school of architecture and design called the Bauhaus, at Weimar, which aimed like Le Corbusier at breaking down the barriers between art and science. The new functionalism taught that decoration should be sub-servient to use for both buildings and everyday objects. The Swiss painter Paul Klee taught at the Bauhaus for the first half of the decade.

Mauler v. Orchid

A BOXING MATCH DUBBED 'the battle of the century' took place in New Jersey in July between world heavy-weight champion Jack Dempsey – 'the Manessa Mauler' – and Georges Carpentier of France, the European champion, nicknamed alternately 'The Orchid Kid' or 'Gorgeous George'. Dempsey knocked Carpentier out for the count in four rounds, but the huge crowd were delighted with what proved to be boxing's first million-dollar promotion.

This is how pupils dressed for games in the 1920s. Note the boys' studded leather boots and the girls' gymslips. Both teams are from Prince Henry's Grammar School in Otley, Yorkshire.

Literary satire

CROME YELLOW, Aldous Huxley's first novel, was a brilliant satire on English high society. Its house-party setting was easily identified as Garsington Manor owned by Lady Ottoline Morrell, free-thinking, literary hostess.

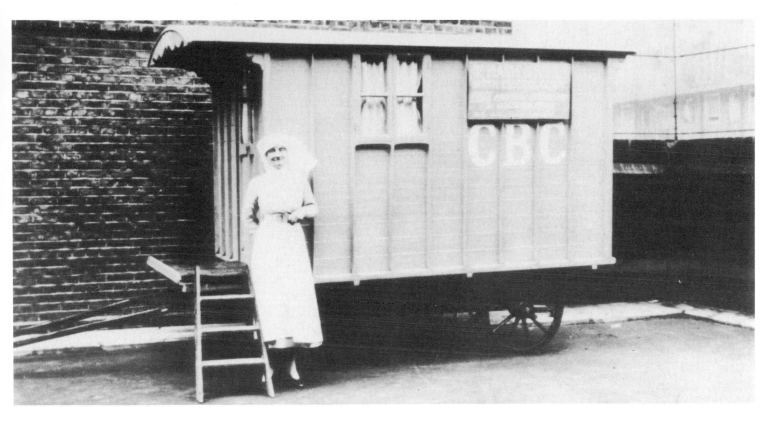

One of Marie Stopes's nurses outside a mobile horse-drawn birth-control clinic.

First birth control clinics

THE MOTHERS' CLINIC, Britain's first birth-contol centre, was opened by Dr Marie Stopes at Holloway in London in March. Dr Stopes started her career as a botanist and became a doctor of science. In 1918 she published two pioneering books – *Married Love* and *Wise Parenthood* – in which she advocated contraception as a means both of improving the quality of married life and of controlling over-population. Though she was against abortion and restricted the sale of contraceptives to married women, she was bitterly opposed by the churches and much of the press. She started the Society for Constructive Birth Control and Radical Progress in August 1922 and in 1923 published a treatise on *Contraception, Its Theory, History and Practice*. She continued to publicize her ideas, to train nurses and to run her clinics throughout the decade.

Nobel prize for physicist

ALBERT EINSTEIN, the physicist whose Theory of Relativity revolutionized scientific thought, was awarded the Nobel Prize for Physics in 1921. In that year also, he published a major work entitled *The Meaning of Relativity*

American pioneer

IN AMERICA, birth-control pioneer Mrs Margaret Sanger had been imprisoned for 'obscenity' in 1916, but in 1921 she founded the American Birth Control League. Two years later she opened a birth control clinic in New York.

Diabetic discovery

DIABETES WAS A KILLER DISEASE until 1921 when two Canadian scientists discovered insulin. This is a substance produced by the pancreas to absorb and convert the glucose from carbohydrates in the body into energy. In diabetics the insulin mechanism is defective. The blood-sugar level continues to rise, causing coma and, eventually, death.

Frederick Banting and Charles Best, working in the University of Toronto, discovered that by injecting a preparation of insulin extracted from animal pancreases into a diabetic patient, the disease could be controlled. Their discovery enabled diabetics to live normal lives with daily injections of insulin and a strict diet.

1922 Fascist dictator

Mussolini pictured with his generals after the March on Rome.

Mussolini takes power

THE MARCH ON ROME in October made Mussolini at once Prime Minister of Italy and the first of Europe's Fascist Dictators. The famous March became a Fascist legend but it was not, on Mussolini's part, actually undertaken on foot. To avoid a violent 'coup', King Vittorio Emanuele III invited him to Rome to take over the government – and Mussolini went by train.

Signor Mussolini left Milan immediately for Rome after being summoned by the King to form a Cabinet. He will arrive in Rome this evening. Signor Mussolini will himself take over the portfolios of Foreign Affairs and Interior in addition to being Prime Minister. His Ministry is already in great part constituted.
Reuter News Agency report

Outside Rome Mussolini met 22,000 of his 'Black Shirt' supporters and led a ceremonial march into the city on 30 October.

Blackshirt violence

THE KING'S ACTION in summoning Mussolini ended months of near civil war in Italy. Serious riots with violent fighting between Blackshirts and their left-wing opponents took place in most major cities, as Fascist strong-arm men beat and burnt their way to power. By the beginning of 1921 Fascists were in control of most of the North and many of the central regions of Italy. In May the party assumed a measure of respectability by gaining 35 seats in the Parliamentary election.

in Italy

Top hat revolution

WHEN THE ITALIAN KING sent for Mussolini to form a Fascist government, *The Spectator*, a British political weekly, noted: '. . . one picturesque touch very characteristic of an Italian revolution. The new Ministers asked their chief as to the clothes they should wear when kissing hands. "Top hats and black coats" was the laconic order of the Prime Minister, though he had to send out one of his colleagues in a hurry to buy him the necessary top hat.'

The Spectator commented: 'Apparently the silken cylinder is to be the symbol of the new Government's policy', and in Europe many politicians indeed felt at first that in his international dealings Mussolini would turn out to be a gentleman.

New policy, new victims

AT FIRST MUSSOLINI HEADED a coalition of Fascists and Nationalists but by the end of November, in spite of a token parliamentary opposition, he was virtually dictator.

Hopes for peace

In telegrams to the British and French Prime Ministers, Mussolini oozed goodwill. On taking power his message to them ran: 'I am confident that. . . I shall be able to safeguard the supreme interests of the country, which are in accordance with the interests of peace and civilization, and that the solidarity of the Allied nations which I regard as indispensable for their political action will be assured.'

Many believed him. Conservative politicians regarded Fascist Italy as a bulwark against Communism; Ramsay MacDonald, the Labour leader, wrote friendly letters to Mussolini. With others, he hoped that Italy's presence in the League of Nations would further the cause of European harmony, and act as a buffer between France and Germany.

The jibe that all Mussolini did was to make the Italian trains run on time was not strictly true. On gaining power he introduced a programme of public works to step up industrial and agricultural production so that the country could be more self-sufficient.

Early victims of the Fascist rule were the left-wing political parties, the trade unions and the free press, all of which were suppressed.

Il Duce

MUSSOLINI WAS A VAIN MAN who delighted in posing in ornate uniforms. His followers called him Il Duce (leader). Though nationalistic, his philosophy had little of the racist frenzy of Nazism and he never managed to subdue completely the Italian opponents of Fascism. He despised parliamentary democracy and believed that with dictatorial powers he could solve Italy's economic problems and put her firmly on the map as a world power. Some people abroad, however, considered him to be a buffoon as well as a bully.

Fascism

THE ITALIAN FASCIST PARTY began as an organization of action groups known as *Fasci di Combattimento*. They took as their emblem the bundle of rods bound round an axe which had been the symbol of state authority in Ancient Rome. Mussolini unified the groups into a national party in 1919, against a background of growing industrial depression and unemployment with which a series of coalition governments seemed powerless to cope.

Disaffected ex-soldiers, many with a taste for violence, joined the paramilitary organization, whose members wore black shirts as part of their uniform. Soon it was supported by right-wing industrialists and land-owners, and by many of the police. Squads of Fascist thugs were trained to beat up opponents, break up left-wing meetings and terrorize working-class communities. Among their 'weapons' were large bottles of castor oil, a powerful and foul-tasting laxative, which they forced their victims to swallow.

Big bluff

MUSSOLINI IS THE BIGGEST BLUFF IN EUROPE. If Mussolini would have me taken out and shot tomorrow morning I would still regard him as a bluff. The shooting would be a bluff. Get hold of a good photo of Signor Mussolini and study it. You will see the weakness in his mouth which forces him to scowl the famous Mussolini scowl that is imitated by every nineteen-year-old fascisto in Italy . . . . And then look at his black shirt and his white spats. There is something wrong, even histrionically, with a man who wears white spats with a black shirt.

Ernest Hemingway in *The Toronto Daily Star*, 27 January 1923

Gandhi in prison

THE INDIAN NATIONALIST LEADER, M.K. Gandhi, was imprisoned in 1922 for his opposition to British rule. A Hindu, whose followers called him 'Mahatma' ('great soul'), he was deeply religious and believed strongly in pacifism and self-denial. He adopted a policy of passive resistance to the British authorities. Many thousands of Indians joined him in his crusade of non-violent civil disobedience.

India had been known as the 'jewel' of the British Empire, but under the India Act of 1919 Britain agreed to work towards Indian self-government. There were serious rifts between the two main religious groups, Hindu and Muslim, but neither regarded the progress towards independence as fast enough. A massacre at Amritsar, in which British troops fired into a crowd and killed nearly 400 people, was the spur for a decade and more of protest.

At his trial for publishing three anti-British articles in his journal *Young India*, Gandhi said:

In my humble opinion, non-cooperation with evil is as much a duty as is cooperation with good .... I am here, therefore, to invite and submit cheerfully to the highest penalty that can be inflicted upon me for what in law is a deliberate crime and what appears to me to be the highest duty of a citizen ....

Gandhi in typical cross-legged pose.

Egypt gains independence

EGYPT, which had been under British rule for 40 years, was declared independent in 1922. Britain retained control of the Sudan. British troops remained in Egypt to guard her interests in the Suez Canal, a vital route to India and the Far East. Egypt's nationalist party, the Wafd, was strongly opposed to this part of the settlement.

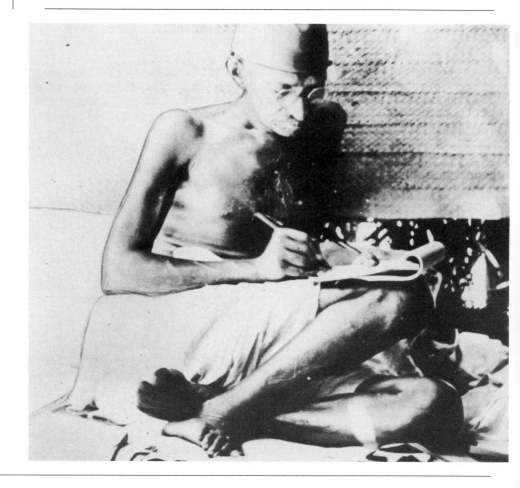

Irish Civil War

IN IRELAND the Dail approved the treaty with Britain by a narrow majority but a bitter civil war broke out. Opponents of the settlement, led by De Valera, fought its supporters – who included Griffith and Collins. This time the IRA was fighting against the new Free State's national army. In April the Republicans seized the Four Courts of Justice in Dublin. The building, along with most of Ireland's state records, was destroyed when Collins's troops counter-attacked.

Collins himself was shot dead in an ambush in August while he was inspecting troops. His prophecy made on the signing of the treaty had come true.

Clashes in Ulster

PARTITION did not bring peace to Northern Ireland either. Nearly 300 people were killed in 1922 in bitter clashes between supporters of the Protestant majority and the Catholic minority. Violent sectarian battles in Belfast and Londonderry led to a Special Powers Act, which gave the government and police sweeping powers of arrest and imprisonment.

Murder case

IN A SENSATIONAL TRIAL at the Old Bailey in December, Edith Thompson and Frederick Bywaters were jointly found guilty of the murder of Mrs Thompson's husband, Percy. Bywaters stabbed him in the street but love letters read out in court showed that the couple had planned the murder together. They were hanged at the same hour on the same day but in different prisons.

Turkish Republic formed

THE ONCE-VAST TURKISH EMPIRE had been split up after the First World War, in which Turkey fought on Germany's side. An area round Smyrna in Asia Minor was ceded to Greece. In 1922 Turkish troops advanced and drove the Greeks out. They then pushed on towards Chanak, held by the British. All-out war was averted by the signing of a pact under which some of Turkey's former territories were restored to her. The Turkish nationalist leader, Mustapha Kemal, deposed the Sultan in November and set up a Turkish Republic. He started to carry out a programme of modernization.

Coalition crisis

LLOYD GEORGE LOST SUPPORT of the Tories in his Cabinet over the Chanak crisis and the coalition government ended in October.

Bonar Law became Prime Minister of a Conservative government but resigned after a few months because of poor health. His successor, Stanley Baldwin, remained at the centre of the political stage until the late 1930s, and was Prime Minister for much of the 1920s. The son of a Worcestershire iron-master, he first became a Conservative MP in 1908. He gained the image of a 'man of the people' and, though a shrewd politician, was always depicted as a contemplative, pipe-smoking family-man.

Government axes spending

FURTHER CUTS IN GOVERNMENT SPENDING followed a report by a committee headed by Sir Eric Geddes, former Transport Minister. The economies, soon known as the 'Geddes axe', affected education, public health, housing and the armed services.

Newspaper war

NEWSPAPER MAGNATE LORD NORTHCLIFFE died in August. He was the founder of Britain's first 'popular' newspaper, the *Daily Mail*, and also owned *The Times*. Before his death he planned a bitter 'circulation war' against other papers with large sales such as the *Daily Express*, owned by the Canadian, Lord Beaverbrook, and the Labour *Daily Herald*. Journalistic 'scoops' took second place as readers were lured with offers of free insurance, gifts of cutlery, clothing, fountain pens or cameras, and even the complete works of Dickens – with bookcase thrown in.

Stanley Baldwin with his wife (right) and daughter.

Wins for champion jockey

THE DERBY, run at Epsom in June, was a day out for thousands of racing enthusiasts from top-hatted 'gents' and fashionable ladies to East End punters and family parties who came by motor bus or coach for a flutter on the big race. Their favourite rider in the first half of the twenties was Steve Donoghue, champion jockey (with most wins in the season) from 1914 to 1923 and six times winner of the Derby.

He won it twice during the war, came first on Humorist in 1921 and again on Captain Cuttle in 1922. He completed the hat-trick the following year when he won again on Papyrus, and had his last win on Manna in 1925. Gordon Richards, who was later knighted, became champion jockey that year for the first time. He held the title 26 times between 1925 and 1953.

Cigarette cards showing Steve Donoghue on some of his winning mounts.

Tarzan's swimming records

AMERICAN SWIMMER JOHNNY WEISSMULLER became the first man to swim 100 metres in under one minute in 1922. Swimming freestyle, he covered the distance in 58.6 seconds. He began breaking records in 1921 at the age of 17 and during his career won 52 US titles and set 28 world distance records. He won three gold medals at the 1924 Olympics and two in 1928. Among sportsmen he became known as 'the greatest swimmer ever' – but to the general public he was much more famous for his portrayal of Tarzan in numerous adventure films.

Waste Land

T.S. ELIOT, one of the most influential poets of the twentieth century, published his first major work, *The Waste Land*, this year. Breaking away from traditional forms, it was written in free verse. It puzzled some readers by its lack of structure, while critics argued – and are still arguing – about its deeper meaning.

Stream of consciousness

ANOTHER MAJOR WRITER of the decade was the Irish author James Joyce, whose controversial novel *Ulysses* was published in 1922 but banned in many countries, including Ireland and England, because of its alleged 'obscene' content. It describes a day in the lives of three Dublin characters and employed some of the 'stream of consciousness' techniques which Joyce later developed more fully in *Finnegans Wake*.

Paris publisher

ULYSSES was published in France by Sylvia Beach, an American who ran a Paris bookshop called Shakespeare & Co. She gave support and encouragement to many struggling writers. One was Ernest Hemingway, who began his career as a journalist and later became a prolific novelist. Two of his early works were *The Sun Also Rises* (1925) and *A Farewell to Arms* (1929).

Egyptian tomb discovered

TUTANKHAMEN'S TOMB near Thebes in Egypt was discovered by archaeologists in 1922. The boy-king's treasure, revealed after more than 3000 years, started a craze for anything Egyptian. Clothes, furnishings and art all followed the fashion.

Broadcasting

THE BRITISH BROADCASTING COMPANY was formed in October and its London station, 2LO, with a staff of four, soon moved to studios at Savoy Hill. The BBC was given the monopoly of broadcasting in Britain and was run as a public service. Advertising was not allowed on it and it received its revenue from the annual wireless licences which people who wanted to 'listen in' had to buy from the Post Office for 10s each.

At the first All-British Wireless Exhibition and Convention in October manufacturers put on show BBC-approved sets. Some were crystal sets with earphones but the more advanced type were powered by valves and had loudspeakers. Valve wirelesses worked off a large dry battery with an accumulator which had to be recharged frequently.

Wireless set

Mary Wade's father was a radio enthusiast and soon replaced his home-made crystal set with a valve one.

In the front bedroom of our house, there stood the main part of our wireless set, and the wires went through the floor to the living room underneath. The receiver was modernized from the headphones (of the crystal set) to a huge black horn . . . . My father was perpetually winding new coils of wire on to a big bobbin affair, but although this was to amplify the sound, it was necessary to stand quite near to the receiver if one wished to be certain of hearing a favourite programme. Neither my sister Frances nor myself cared much for taking the glass accumulator to the nearest garage for recharging, as it was filled with acid, and could do a deal of damage to the skin or clothing if it was not carried very carefully.
Mary Wade, *To the Miner Born*

Austin produces baby car

THE INTRODUCTION OF THE AUSTIN SEVEN, a four-cylinder, four-seater car with a three-speed gearbox, made British motoring history. Henry Ford had been mass-producing the Model 'T' in America since 1914 and in Britain the 'Bullnose' Morris was a popular car during the same period. But the 'Baby Austin' brought car-owning within the reach of many middle-class people who had previously been unable to afford it.

The manufacturer, Herbert Austin, put it on the market in July at £165. He described it as 'a decent car for the man who, at present, can only afford a motorcycle and sidecar and yet has the ambition to become a motorist'. Petrol was then around 1s 6d a gallon, driving licences – with no test – were 5s each, and insurance was optional. Families took to the 'open road' with enthusiasm.

The Austin 7 which came on the market this year.

1923 Collapse of the

France occupies Ruhr

FRENCH TROOPS marched into the Ruhr, Germany's main industrial area, in January. The occupation was in protest against Germany's failure to pay reparations, and in particular to meet promised deliveries of coal.

Essen, Thursday
At an early hour this morning strong French forces entered the Ruhr region, and about 10 o'clock had reached the outskirts of Essen. Thus begins another chapter in the cobbled history of Central Europe. All yesterday . . . all sorts of rumours were flying about and the streets were crowded. A great mass meeting of protest was held, and people, mainly students, paraded the streets singing patriotic songs . . . . Considerable numbers of people waited in the station square all night, in the expectation of seeing the French troops arrive. It must have been about 4 o'clock when the French columns – cavalry, infantry, tanks and artillery, moved off from the Dusseldorf bridgehead . . . on route towards Essen, the world-famous centre of the Krupp works and the economic heart of Germany's industrial region.
Daily Chronicle, 12 January

Opposition

BELGIUM AGREED with French Prime Minister Raymond Poincaré that full reparations should be paid but Britain and America opposed the occupation. Realizing the impossibility of Germany ever paying such vast debts, their governments felt that economic help for the defeated country was more important.

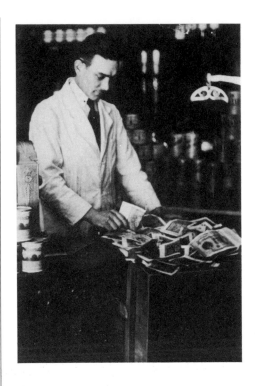

German protests

THE OCCUPATION was bitterly resented by the Germans, who resisted it whenever and wherever they could – with sabotage and riots, street fighting and attacks on French soldiers. Coal production stopped altogether because miners went on strike.

We have long said in the Ruhr you can do nearly everything with a bayonet – except pick coal. Herr Poincaré has yet to learn that the pick wielded by the free German workman anxious to do his share to fulfil his country's obligations is a better producer of reparation coal than the bayonet.
From speech by Ruhr trade unionist

As German inflation soared, the shopkeeper's till became too small to hold all the notes. This grocer has put his takings in a tea-chest.

Fall of the mark

THE MARK, Germany's unit of currency, fell in value so dramatically after the occupation that very soon it was totally worthless. From the pre-war standard rate of four marks to the dollar, it had fallen by July to 160,000 to the dollar. In August it was one million and by November a staggering 130,000 million marks were needed to match one dollar.

The collapse of the currency meant total ruin for German trade and industry. German businessmen went bankrupt, savings were wiped out overnight, prices soared and the workers faced unemployment and near starvation. Government presses issued paper notes like falling leaves in a hurricane and overprinted old notes and postage stamps with rows and rows of zeroes. People took their money to the shops in suitcases and barrows. Thousands of bank notes loaded into a baby's pram would just buy one loaf of bread.

Disorders broke out all over Germany as everyone, from the Communists on the left to the supporters of the National Socialist (Nazi) party on the extreme right, protested against the grim situation. A coalition came into power to save Germany's democratic government, the Weimar Republic, which had been created in 1919. The new Chancellor (head of government) was Gustav Stresemann, who later achieved note as Foreign Minister.

Deutschmark

Beer hall putsch

SQUADS OF ARMED 'STORM-TROOPERS' burst into a political meeting in a beer-hall on the outskirts of Munich in November. Firing a pistol in the air, their leader Adolf Hitler pushed aside the speaker and declared:

The National Revolution has begun. This hall is occupied by 600 heavily armed men. No one may leave the hall. The Bavarian and Reich governments have been removed and a provisional National Government formed. The army and police barracks have been occupied, troops and police are marching on the city under the swastika banner.
Quoted in Alan Bullock, *Hitler, a Study in Tyranny*

With the former war leader Erich von Ludendorff beside him, Hitler led his troops into the centre of Munich. They were fired on by a cordon of police and the march broke up when 16 marchers were killed. Hermann Goering, one of Hitler's chief supporters, was badly wounded.

This attempt to seize power by force was planned as the first stage of a nationalist takeover, which was to end with a march on Berlin. After the confrontation in Munich the Putsch petered out. Hitler was arrested, tried for treason and sent to jail.

Storm Troopers

THE NAZI PARTY had its own strong-arm squads which were used to attack Communists and Social Democrats, beat up Jews, and to keep order at mass meetings. The members of the *Sturm Abteilung* (storm troopers), which was known as the SA, wore brown uniforms with strong leather jackboots and armbands emblazoned with the party symbol. This was a swastika, or crooked cross, which had been adapted from an ancient lucky sign.

This poster warns 'Germany is occupied by enemies'.

Nazi Party

LIKE MUSSOLINI IN ITALY, Adolf Hitler had no faith in the ability of Germany's democratic government to solve the economic crisis and lead the country back to a position of power in the world. After service in the war as an Army Corporal, he joined the tiny German Workers' Party, which advocated a mixture of nationalism and socialism. In 1920 he changed its name to National Socialist German Workers' Party, and became its President in 1921. Now known as the Nazi Party, it had become more nationalist than socialist though some aims, such as the nationalization of key industries, were retained.

Nazi centre

Bavaria in Southern Germany was once a kingdom and after the 1914-18 war still had its own state government, and its own elected assembly. In the 1920s it became the centre of German nationalism and a fruitful ground for Nazi converts. The Nazi Party was born in the Bavarian capital, Munich, and another Bavarian city, Nuremburg, became the setting for the party's annual mass rallies.

Ceasefire in Ireland

CIVIL WAR IN IRELAND ended in May. De Valera, however, still regarded himself as head of a Republican government and he and Sinn Fein remained opposed to the settlement with Britain. The Irish Free State, as it was now called, settled down to an uneasy peace under its President, William Cosgrave. That year it became a member of the League of Nations.

Klan terror in America

THE KU KLUX KLAN, an American secret society founded in the Southern states to uphold 'white supremacy', was very active in the 1920s, with a membership of nearly five million. It carried out a campaign of terror against blacks who were still segregated from whites in the South and suffered from widespread racial discrimination. The Klan was also against Catholics, Jews and foreigners. It ran a campaign against the Democratic Party's Presidential candidate, Alfred E. Smith, who was a Catholic.

Klan members wore white hoods with eye-slits and carried out elaborate initiation ceremonies.

White robes hide the identity of Ku Klux Klan members, shown here beside their symbolic cross.

On the other side . . . was a circle of white-robed figures enclosing a space of perhaps three or four acres. To the east of it rose against the moonlit sky the poles of a cross, the upright apparently 60 feet high. Beneath it was a rostrum. On it stood an imposing white-robed figure . . . the Exalted Cyclops . . . . In the center of the great ring was an altar at which another robed figure stood. The Exalted Cyclops addressed him as 'Nighthawk' . . . . The 'aliens' were massed across the altar from the cross, and oaths and obligations were read to them, to which they swore successively with their right hands on their hearts and their left hands uplifted. Those who followed the reading of the pledges noted that they emphasized especially 'white supremacy' . . . . At the end of a prayer the great cross was lighted . . . . The upright and the arm to the south blazed up so that they were seen, it was learned later, seven miles away. The north arm merely smouldered . . . .'
New York World, 3 May

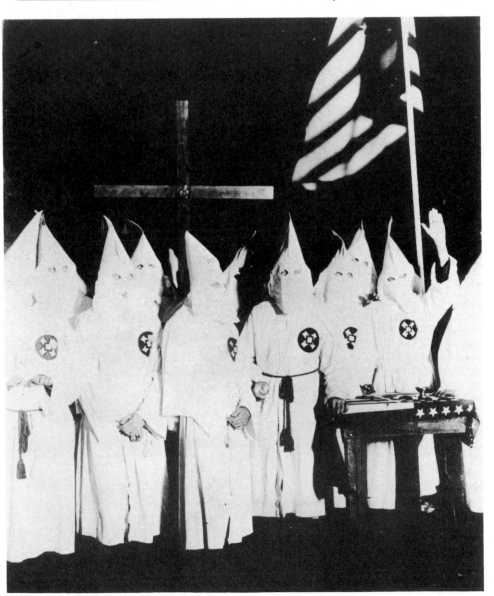

Royal wedding

WITHIN THE STATELY SPLENDOUR OF Westminster Abbey, the Duke of York and Lady Elizabeth Bowes-Lyon became man and wife today. The sun broke through the clouds even as they spoke their marriage vows – an omen, as many said, of future happiness.
The Sphere, 26 April 1923

The Duke of York was George V's second son. His elder brother Edward was never crowned King because he abdicated in 1936. The Duke then became King George VI.

Domestic service

FOR MANY GIRLS, especially in areas of high unemployment, the only chance of getting a job was still, as in pre-war days, to apply to 'go into service' as a housemaid.

Often, at 14 years of age, they went long distances from home and lived with their employer. Free time was limited to one afternoon per week, and at all other times the 'mistress' insisted on housemaids wearing morning and afternoon uniforms, blue dresses with white cap and apron for mornings, and black with a fancy cap and apron was worn when the dirty work was completed.

Mary Wade, *To the Miner Born*

Newspaper ads:

Housemaid wanted. Under-maid kept. five in family. Good refs essential.

Required at once, a young girl to train as housemaid.

Cook-general and young house-parlourmaid wanted. Own bedrooms. No basement. Good wages. Good outings. Four in family.

Parlour maid post vacant. Three in family. Three other maids kept. Good refs essential.

The Duke and Duchess of York taking a stroll on their honeymoon.

Women's freedom

THE MATRIMONIAL CAUSES ACT, giving women equal rights in divorce cases, was passed in 1923 – one more achievement in the fight for feminine emancipation. In the twenties the position of women was remarkably different to that of pre-war years.

The carnage of the war meant that there were now two million more women in Britain than men. People unkindly called them 'surplus women', because there were not enough young men to go round in the 'marriage market'. During the war, however, women had successfully done 'men's jobs' such as working in factories and driving ambulances, and they were fired with a new spirit of freedom.

Women over 30 now had the vote and the first woman MP, Nancy Astor, took her seat in 1920. Though the number of women students was far below that of men, they were treated equally at all universities except Oxford and Cambridge and most of the professions were open to them – though it often took some determination to get in. At offices the woman typist or secretary was rapidly replacing the male clerk and more and more salesgirls were seen behind shop counters. Independent women were given a new title – 'bachelor girls'.

Young Lady with experience of filing and knowledge of shorthand and typing required for important business. Salary, 17s 6d.
Lady clerk required. Good short-hand typist and quick at figures.
(Newspaper 'sits-vac' ads.)

Crazes

CROSSWORD PUZZLES first appeared in books in America in 1923 and by the following year, when newspapers started printing them as 'crossword squares', they were 'all the rage' in Britain. Other crazes of the era were pogo-sticks and the Chinese parlour game of Mah-Jong.

Sport and the Arts

Curious Uncles

THE FIRST ISSUE OF THE *RADIO TIMES*, the BBC's weekly magazine, was published on 28 September at a price of 2d. It contained daily details of talks, musical recitals, news bulletins and other programmes. *Children's Hour*, which started in October, was a popular success and had, like most of the early programmes, an endearing informality about it – for one thing, it was not even an hour long. It was run by a team of jovial 'uncles' and later 'aunts' as well. In an article which he started with the words 'By Jove, everybody!' Uncle Caractacus (C.A. Lewis) wrote this about them in the *Radio Times* in October:

An 'Uncle' is a curious creature . . . . He is a man, in most cases a young man, who has been worried with a thousand and one things pertinent to broadcasting programmes all day long; but when the mystic hour strikes, he casts off his robes of state, takes a deep breath and becomes an – 'Uncle' . . . . He's an intimate relation to thousands of children of all ages, most of whom he has never seen and never will see. He has to 'get over' to 'listeners' by voice, and voice alone . . . . He radiates, or should radiate, understanding, sympathy, good-fellowship, great-heartedness . . . .

BBC's top man

JOHN REITH, the BBC's first general manager, was made managing director in 1923. He was knighted in 1927. A dour and puritanical Scotsman, he had a profound influence on broadcasting which he believed 'should bring into the greatest possible number of homes . . . all that is best in every department of human knowledge, endeavour and achievement'. Of paramount importance was the preservation of a 'high moral tone'.

The captains of the FA Cup Final teams waiting for the police to clear the crowds. Bolton's captain is on the right.

Riot at Cup Final

THE NEW WEMBLEY STADIUM, completed in 1923, was the setting for the Football Association Cup Final that year, an event marred by a near-riot on the pitch. More than 100,000 people bought tickets for the match between Bolton Wanderers and West Ham United, but the numbers inside the ground were doubled when thousands stormed the turnstiles. It took police 40 minutes to restore order so that the game could start. A thousand people were injured in the mêlée. The hero of the day was a policeman on a white horse who helped to push the excited football fans off the pitch. Bolton won the match 2-0.

Railway 'Big Four' formed

BRITAIN'S RAILWAY COMPANIES had been run by the government during the war but afterwards it was decided to amalgamate the dozens of different lines into four large groups, still privately owned but with a monopoly in their own areas. The 'grouping' came into effect on 1 Jan, 1923, creating a 'Big Four' of the Great Western, the Southern, the London Midland & Scottish and the London & North Eastern railways.

Steam engines were becoming faster and more powerful. The LMS, with its star runner the *Royal Scot* and the LNER, with the famous *Flying Scotsman* locomotive, became rivals in a race to provide the fastest service from London to Scotland. In 1928 the *Flying Scotsman* became the first to do a regular non-stop run from London to Edinburgh in 8½ hours.

Immunization and isolation

DISEASES like smallpox and diphtheria were still a serious scourge in the 1920s. Epidemics spread through whole communities, killing many.

Though a smallpox vaccine had been discovered more than a century earlier, it was not widely used. Immunization against diphtheria was introduced in 1923 at the same time as injections against tetanus. Tuberculosis was still widespread, especially in the un-hygienic conditions of overcrowded slums. Scarlet fever remained prevalent among children throughout the decade. As with diphtheria, this meant a long stay in hospital. At home the patient's bedroom was fumigated. Clothes, books and other possessions which might be harbouring the germs were either burnt or taken away for decontamination.

When 10-year-old Lena Wilson woke up one morning with a sore throat and a rash, scarlet fever was diagnosed and she was hurried off by ambulance for 'six weeks in isolation'.

I suppose it was clean and well organized but as living accommodation for up to sixteen children for six weeks the ward was stark . . . . The programme of therapy was simple. For the first week we had nothing to eat; the policy of 'starve a fever' was carried out to the letter. Twice a day we were given some bitter medicine and, on the morning round, our throats were brushed with iodine . . . . Apart from our cautious progress to soft foods in the second week, a combination of throat tickling and quinine seemed to produce the desired result . . . . Parents were not allowed to see the patients but they could visit the hospital each afternoon to make enquiries in the small waiting room near the main entrance. There they could leave parcels and letters . . . . Mother came every day.
The Sunshine Casts No Shadow

Health care

THERE WAS NO NATIONAL HEALTH SERVICE in the 1920s. Local authorities ran fever hospitals and tuberculosis sanatoriums and made provision for women in childbirth. Hospital care for other cases was organized on a patchwork basis by private bodies, charities and voluntary organizations and by the Poor Law administration. Those in employment received help with medical care on their national insurance and the Ministry of Health arranged medical checks for school children. Many families paid regular contributions to a hospital fund but many more had to fall back on public assistance in times of illness.

The LNER's chief engineer, Nigel Gresley, designed a corridor-tender for the Flying Scotsman *so engine crews could be changed on a non-stop run from London to Edinburgh. Here a member of the relief crew walks through to the footplate.*

DAILY HERALD

LATE LONDON EDITION

To-Day's Weather

Wind S.E., light or moderate. Rain early, then fairer temporarily mist. Moderate temperature.

No. 2,488 (No. 1,495—New Series)   LONDON, WEDNESDAY, JANUARY 23, 1924.   ONE PENNY

FIRST BRITISH LABOUR CABINET

MR. MACDONALD NOW PREMIER

Rapid Developments Follow on Mr. Baldwin's Resignation

AUDIENCES WITH THE KING

Three Peers in the Government : Admiralty Provides a Surprise

The announcement of the constitution of a Labour Cabinet, the first in this country, followed closely, yesterday, on Mr. Baldwin's resignation and Mr. MacDonald's undertaking to form a Government.

The list, which includes the names of three peers (Lords Haldane, Parmoor, and Chelmsford), and three commoners without seats in the House (Mr. Arthur Henderson, Sir Sydney Olivier and Brigadier-General C. B. Thomson), contains many surprises.

The appointments of Ministers not in the Cabinet and Under-Secretaries will be announced later.

WHY CABINET IS LARGE ONE

Plans for Working on Business-like Lines

MEETING TO-DAY

The first meeting of the new Cabinet will be held at 10, Downing-street, at 4 p.m. to-day (writes our Lobby Correspondent).

The great, and, I believe, unprecedented promptitude with which the new Cabinet has been announced and is taking over the Administration has created a very favourable impression.

The filling up of the Under-Secretaryships is, I am able to state, almost completed, and a full announcement may be expected in a day or two. I believe it will be found that the new Minister of Mines is Mr. Shinwell.

The Cabinet will be a large one. The reason for this it that a great deal of the work will be done by Committees of Ministers.

Three committees will thresh out the questions referred to them and report their conclusions to the full Cabinet, the functions of which will be to supervise and make the final decisions. Thus the country will have for the first time a Government

RAIL STRIKE LEADERS PROPOSE PARLEY

But Managers Insist on Acceptance of Wages Board's Award

"DISCUSS DIFFERENCES"
—Loco Union's Offer

Correspondence passed yesterday between the railway managers and the Associated Society, whose members are on strike. The managers, while prepared to meet the men's leaders, repeated their insistence on acceptance of the Wages Board's award.

The Executive of the Associated Society replied by reiterating its willingness to meet the managers to discuss the adjustment of differences.

"N.U.R. men in all parts of the country are joining us," said an A.S.L.E. and F. official last night. Other statements by union officials, and reports from strike areas, are printed on Page Three.

INDUSTRY SLOWS DOWN

LENIN DIES SUDDENLY

POIGNANT SCENE IN THE SOVIET

A LONG SILENCE

MOSCOW MOURNS GREAT LEADER

Nicolai Lenin (Vladimir Ilyitch Oulianoff) died at 6.50 on Monday evening at Gorky, in the hills near Moscow.

He had seemed to be recovering from his long illness—the aftermath of his attempted assassination in 1918; but suddenly on Monday afternoon he became worse. Paralysis of the respiratory organs set in. At 5.30 breathing became difficult. He lost consciousness, and died at 6.50.

The All-Russian Soviet Congress was in session yesterday morning at the Bolshoi Theatre in Moscow, when Kalenin—the President of the Republic—tears streaming down his face—told

Labour's paper, the Daily Herald, *announces the historic election win.*

Workers' cabinet for Britain

BRITAIN'S FIRST LABOUR GOVERNMENT took office in January, headed by James Ramsay MacDonald, who combined the posts of Prime Minister and Foreign Secretary. It was the country's first-ever Cabinet composed of mainly working-class men. It included Philip Snowden, the son of a Yorkshire weaver, J.H. Thomas, the railwaymen's leader, and Arthur Henderson, a former iron worker. In a letter to his

Non-socialist programme

LABOUR HAD LITTLE CHANCE, however, of carrying out a socialist programme. It was a minority government, only kept in power by the support of the Liberals. In the general election of the previous December the Conservatives had won 258 seats and Labour 191. So

mother, George V wrote: 'They have different ideas to ours as they are all socialists, but they ought to be given a chance and ought to be treated fairly.'

the Liberal party with 158 MPs held the balance of power in the House of Commons. The Tories could not form a government without Liberal support, which was not given; Labour could only govern with it.

MacDonald settled for a moderate programme of social reforms, including more council house building, better unemployment benefits, higher pensions and various public works schemes to try to cut down unemployment.

in power

Zinoviev letter starts Red scare

The Labour government lasted less than a year. In October the country was once again in the throes of a general election. The campaign was dominated by a 'Red Scare'. While in office the Labour government had decided to give official recognition to Communist Russia. MacDonald had signed a trade agreement with the Soviet government and was negotiating a second agreement which meant that Britain would give Russia a financial loan.

Conservative politicians and the Tory press lambasted him as a 'communist sympathizer'. Then, five days before polling day, the *Daily Mail* published a copy of a letter which, it was claimed, was from Gregori Zinoviev, President of the Communist International, to the British Communist Party. It spoke of the proletarian revolution which would take place in Britain once the Soviet treaty was signed. Communists were urged to prepare for it by persuading members of the armed forces to refuse to fight against working class rebels.

A copy of the letter had been sent to the Foreign Office and read by MacDonald earlier in the month. Its publication on 25 October sealed the fate of the Labour party at the election. 'We're sunk', said J.H. Thomas when he saw the headlines.

> The country now knows that *Moscow issues orders to the British Communists*, and they are obeyed by the Communists here. The *British Communists, in turn, give orders to the Socialist Government which it tamely and humbly obeys* . . . .
>
> Mr MacDonald is betraying the British nation. He is the stalking horse under cover of whom the Reds are plotting the ruin of this country.
>
> *Daily Mail* leading article, 25 October

ON THE LOAN TRAIL.

Punch *depicted a hairy Bolshevik as one of Labour's election supporters. The underlying message was that a vote for Labour was a vote for Russian domination.*

Voters' panic

THE 'RED LETTER' caused an anti-socialist panic among middle class voters and the Conservatives won the election with a resounding 419 seats. Labour gained only 151 and the Liberal share of MPs dropped to 42.

The truth about the Zinoviev letter remains a mystery but it is now thought to have been a forgery. Zinoviev denied writing it and the original was never discovered. Only translated copies were sent out.

Labour's rise to power

THE LABOUR PARTY grew from a Labour Representation Committee which was formed in 1900 to try to get working class MPs elected to the House of Commons. The LRC was an amalgamation of several left-wing groups including the trade unions and the Independent Labour Party, a radical-socialist group formed by Keir Hardie in 1893. In 1906, when the LRC won 29 seats in the general election, it was renamed the Labour Party. In 1918 it adopted a constitution drawn up by the Fabian Society socialist, Sidney Webb. This committed it

> to secure for the producers by hand and by brain the full fruits of their industry, and the most equitable distribution thereof that may be possible, on the basis of the common ownership of the means of production . . . .

Though it was able to form minority governments in 1924 and 1929, it was not until the 'landslide' victory in 1945 that Labour was returned with a big enough parliamentary majority to put this policy into effect by nationalizing the major industries.

MacDonald

BORN IN 1866, RAMSAY MACDONALD was the illegitimate son of a Scottish farm labourer. He was brought up by his mother in acute poverty in the fishing village of Lossiemouth. With a gift for oratory and a flair for organization, he became the first secretary of the LRC and was elected to Parliament in 1906. A pacifist during the war, he lost his seat in 1918 but was re-elected in 1922.

Death of Lenin

VLADIMIR ILYICH LENIN, Russian revolutionary leader and architect of the Soviet Union, died on 21 January at his home in Gorki.

The All-Russian Soviet Congress was in session yesterday morning at the Bolshoi theatre in Moscow, when Kalenin – the President of the Republic – tears streaming down his face – told the news. The great assembly rose and stood for five minutes in silence, very many of them weeping. And from the theatre word spread through Moscow . . . .
Daily Herald, 23 January

Lenin's body was embalmed and taken to Moscow to lie in state. In the freezing cold of a Russian winter – 30C below zero – vast crowds queued in Red Square for a last sight of their leader. In four days, 900,000 filed past the open coffin.

Born in Simbirsk on the middle Volga in 1870, Lenin spent much of his life in exile after being imprisoned by the Tsarist government for revolutionary activities. He returned to Russia in 1917 to lead the Bolshevik Revolution. In the six years before his death he ensured the survival of the world's first Marxist state, which adopted the name Union of Soviet Socialist Republics (USSR) in 1922. His death set the stage for a battle for power between Stalin and Trotsky.

New plan for reparations

CO-OPERATION BETWEEN NATIONS seemed a possibility after the Dawes Report, which proposed that reparations should be paid by Germany on a scale worked out in proportion to her economic recovery. It also said that she should be helped with a financial loan. At an international conference in London in August the plan was accepted and soon afterwards French troops were withdrawn from the Ruhr.

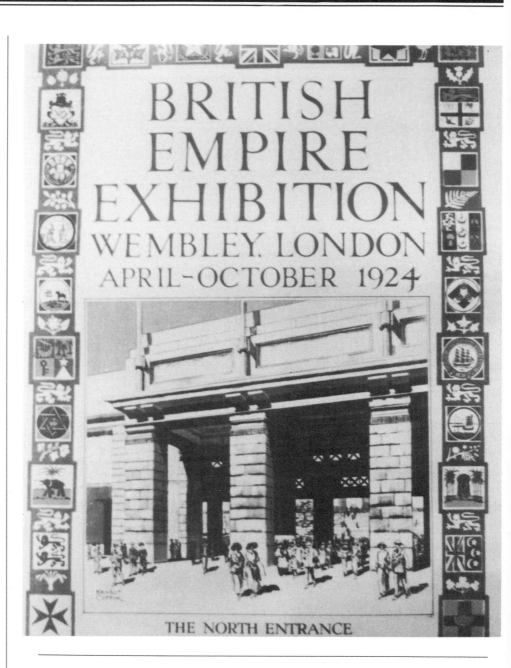

THE NORTH ENTRANCE

Murder in Italy

GIACOMO MATTEOTTI, an Italian socialist leader who had denounced Mussolini's party in a book called *The Fascists Exposed*, was kidnapped and murdered by Fascist thugs in June. There was an outcry in the Italian parliament, but all opposition was ineffective because of a new electoral law. This gave the Fascists – the party with the largest number of votes at the general election that year – two thirds of the seats.

The seal was now set on Mussolini's dictatorship and from then on he proceeded to put into effect what he called 'our fierce totalitarian will'. By 1926 all political opposition was outlawed.

Empire Exhibition

AT WEMBLEY A VAST COMPLEX was built to house the British Empire Exhibition, which was opened by George V in April to the strains of Elgar's *Land of Hope and Glory*. 'We hope that the success of the Exhibition may bring lasting benefit not to the Empire only, but to mankind in general', said the King in a speech which was relayed round the world by wireless.

The exhibition was the largest Britain had ever staged. There were Palaces of Engineering, Industry and Arts, Pavilions from India, Australia, New Zealand, Canada, South Africa, East Africa and the Gold Coast. The New Zealand display boasted real Maoris but the Canadian one capped

A poster for the Wembley exhibition (left).

that with a life-size statue of the Prince of Wales – carved out of butter! Especially popular were the floodlit gardens and a Hong Kong Chinese restaurant, a novelty in Britain then. In the Amusements Park the dodgems were run by a young showman called Billy Butlin, later to become the pioneer of holiday camps.

Farm life

IN BRITAIN, life on the land for farmer and farm worker alike was hard in the 1920s. From 1917 to 1921 the government had guaranteed the farmer a minimum price for his corn. That year – just when the price of wheat was dropping dramatically – the guarantee was scrapped. Hard hit by the slump, many farmers went bankrupt. Those who could turned from arable to dairy farming and, as Britain's arable acreage dropped, milk production went up.

Also scrapped in 1921 was the Agricultural Wages Board, set up to fix minimum wage levels for agricultural workers. Inevitably, farm labourers' wages started to drop. From a minimum of 46s a week in 1920 they went down in some cases as low as 26s. In 1923 farm workers in Norfolk were offered 24s for a 50-hour week – and they went on strike. Eventually they had to settle for 25s but in 1924 the Wages Board was brought back and pay started to rise. For the rest of the decade it stayed at around 30s a week.

Underwear like this was a revolutionary change from the boned corsets and stiff 'foundation garments' of Edwardian days.

Farm mechanization

TRACTORS HAD BEEN TRIED ON FARMS during the war and in the 1920s cost around £120 to buy. Horses remained the chief source of agricultural power, however, for many years to come. The combine harvester appeared in Britain in 1926 but for most farmers mechanization was a luxury they just could not afford.

Master's debut in daring play

NOEL COWARD, whose gifts as playwright, lyricist and actor-manager later earned him the accolade 'Master', first made his name in 1924 when his play *The Vortex* shocked theatre-goers by daring to expose the problem of drug addiction. The play, in which Coward also acted the leading part, became a West End hit. He followed this with another successful play, *Hay Fever*, the following year.

Coward also wrote the lyrics for Charles Cochrane's 1925 revue *On With the Dance* which included the song *Poor Little Rich Girl*. Cochrane's high-kicking chorus line, known as Mr Cochrane's Young Ladies, was a popular feature of West End entertainment throughout the decade.

Shaw play

GEORGE BERNARD SHAW'S historical drama *St Joan* was first produced in 1924, with Sybil Thorndike in the title role. In the following year Shaw was awarded the Nobel Prize for literature.

Musical hit

RHAPSODY IN BLUE by George Gershwin was first performed by Paul Whiteman's orchestra in New York in 1924, and swept the world. It presented jazz in a highly orchestrated form and was said by the music critic of the *New York World* to have 'made an honest woman out of jazz'. In 1930 Gershwin had another success with the jazz-opera *Porgy and Bess*.

Olympic Golds

BRITISH COMPETITORS thrilled their compatriots by winning three gold medals in the athletics events at the Paris Olympics. Harold Abrahams came first in the 100 metres, beating the American sprinter Charley Paddock who was known as 'the world's fastest human', and setting a new Olympic record of 10.6 seconds.

Scotland's Eric Liddell set both the Olympic and world records when he won the 400 metres in 47.6 sec. Douglas Lowe won the 800 metres in 1924 and again in 1928.

One of the heroes of the 1924 Olympics was the Finnish runner Paavo Nurmi, who won 'golds' in four events. Lap times were not called out to distance runners in the 1920s so Nurmi, who liked to run a tactical race, carried a watch in his left hand. During the 3000 metres steeplechase in 1928 he fell in the water-jump, damaged the watch and finished second.

British become 'Lions'

The British Rugby Union side received their nickname, the Lions, during a tour of South Africa in 1924, because of the symbol on their team tie.

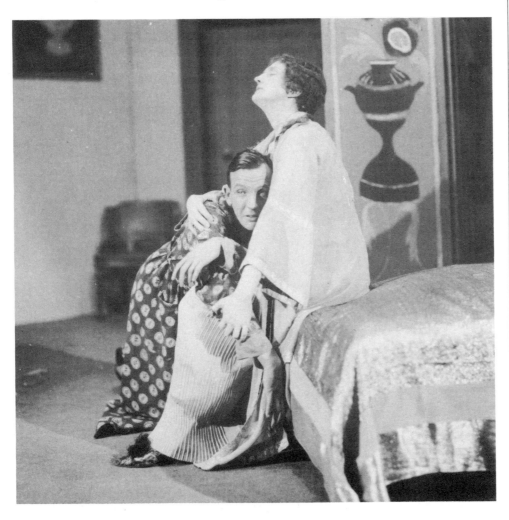
Noel Coward with co-star Lilian Braithwaite in a scene from The Vortex.

Passenger airways

IMPERIAL AIRWAYS WAS FORMED IN 1924, by an amalgamation of several small airlines in Britain. It received a subsidy from the government, which in return had the right to appoint some of the directors. It ran daily air services from London to Paris, Cologne, Zurich and the Channel Islands. Passengers could fly three times a week to Amsterdam and Berlin.

To begin with the aircraft were mostly biplanes and the passengers sat in a cabin underneath the top wing. Gradually these were replaced by faster monoplanes. Private flying clubs, whose members regarded flying as an exciting new sport, used biplanes of the Gypsy Moth type, in which the pilot sat in an open cockpit.

Aircraft were still regarded by many as highly dangerous – more so, surprisingly, than airships. Some thought they should be banned and in 1924 the eminent novelist, John Galsworthy, suggested in a letter to *The Times* that they should not be allowed 'for any purpose whatsoever'. Nothing, however, could stop the development of passenger air travel.

Airport

LONDON'S MAIN AIRPORT was Croydon. *The Book About Aircraft*, published by Frederick Warne, explained that:

Croydon is the most important aerodrome in England, and here there are large booking offices, customs houses, and all the arrangements that are usually found at a seaport. It is called for this reason an airport. The aeroplanes line up on the 'tarmac', that is the flat pavement in front of the offices, to take their passengers. They start off with the regularity of trains at a signal from the control tower . . . (which) has a view all round, and in it there are wireless operators and a large map on which the positions of the liners going to and from Croydon are shown by flags. Each aeroplane is spoken to by wireless every few minutes . . . .

Racing car success

ONE OF THE MOST SUCCESSFUL RACING cars of all time, the Bugatti Type 35, was produced in France in 1924 and went on to win numerous Grand Prix and lesser races during the decade. By now many racing cars were being built with supercharged engines and speeds rose rapidly towards the 150 mph mark.

Brooklands, near Weybridge in Surrey, was Britain's only racing circuit during the period and at the first RAC Grand Prix there in 1926 a 24-litre Napier Railton set a lap record of

> **Useful to Know in Sick Nursing. A good remedy for a cold is to spread a piece of brown paper with pig's lard, then sprinkle over sulphur, and wear over chest.**
> *Tried Favourites Cookery Book*, 1924

143.44 mph. The oval Brooklands track, laid out in 1907 in the shape of a racecourse for horses, was steeply banked and made of concrete. It provided plenty of 'thrills and spills' for the crowds in what was becoming a popular spectator sport.

'Ready for the off' at Brooklands.

The Roaring

Charleston reaches Europe

IN 1925, AT THE MID-POINT of the decade, the Charleston, a flamboyant dance that required high spirits and high kicking, reached Europe from America. Denounced at first by the staid and straightlaced, it seemed to represent all that was lighthearted and outrageous about an era which was called 'The Roaring Twenties'. Dancers abandoned the fox-trot and the waltz to do the Charleston which, especially after it was taken up by the Prince of Wales, became all the rage. It, and another American dance, the Black Bottom, were copied energetically at night-clubs, tea-dances and even village 'hops'.

Flappers flout convention

SOCIALLY THIS WAS THE AGE of the 'flapper', a young woman who went to parties without a chaperone, smoked cigarettes, used lipstick, drove cars, spoke in slang, discussed 'free love' and even swore – all things which would have been unthinkable in Edwardian days. Required reading was *The Green Hat*, melodramatic novel by Michael Arlen, which depicted the unconventional life of the 'gay twenties' and became a best-seller on both sides of the Atlantic. The heroine, Iris Storm, was based on the socialite Nancy Cunard, who later scandalized conventional society by becoming the lover of a black jazz musician. A stage version of *The Green Hat* was put on in London in 1925, with American actress Tallulah Bankhead in the starring role.

Party-going and the Bright Young Things

LONDON NEWSPAPERS were full of the exploits of the 'Bright Young Things', who spent their time in night-clubs and at wild parties, vying with each other to shock the older generation. One of them was Brian Howard. He once set the Thames on fire by pouring gallons of petrol on the water and on another occasion led a chain of leap-frogging friends over the counters at Selfridges department store.

The sort of parties the Bright Young Things went to were listed by the writer Evelyn Waugh in his novel about the twenties, *Vile Bodies*.

. . . . **Masked parties, Savage parties, Victorian parties, Greek parties, Wild West parties, Russian parties, Circus parties, parties where one had to dress as somebody else, almost naked parties in St John's Wood, parties in flats and studios and houses and ships and hotels and nightclubs, in windmills and swimming baths . . . all that succession and repetition of massed humanity . . . . Those vile bodies . . . .**

High spirits at a 'Bright Young Things' party.

Twenties

Night clubs raided

NIGHT CLUBS FLOURISHED in the West End of London. The Bright Young Things could dance and drink from midnight to dawn at the '43 Club, the Silver Slipper, The Manhattan, the Hambone, the Cave of Harmony and many others. Often the clubs were raided by police for selling drinks after licensing hours. One of the most successful night-club owners, Mrs Kate 'Ma' Meyrick, was sent to prison for bribing a member of the vice squad.

Playboy Prince

THE LEADER OF HIGH SOCIETY was the bachelor Prince of Wales. King George V's eldest son, known as David to his family, was often to be seen at the Embassy or the Kit Kat Club, accompanied by a society belle. During a trip to America he was described by *Vanity Fair* magazine as:

. . . the indestructable Dancing Drinking Tumbling Kissing Walking Talking and Sleeping – but not Marrying – idol of the British Empire.
Quoted in Graham Mitchell, *The Roaring Twenties*.

The Prince was a leader of fashion, and a lover of fast cars and dangerous sports such as steeplechasing. He had his serious side, however, and spent many months travelling to 'outposts' of the Empire such as India, and Australia. He also tried to 'meet the people' in Britain and showed concern about the plight of the unemployed in the North and in South Wales. 'Some of the things I see in their gloomy, poverty-stricken areas make me almost ashamed to be an Englishman' he said.

Fashion decrees short skirts

FULL EVENING DRESS was worn in London society after dark but, by day, clothes were more informal than ever before. Women's skirts which in 1920 had been ankle-length, had risen by mid-decade up to the knee. Cecil Beaton, the photographer, described the typical mid-twenties woman in his book *The Glass of Fashion*. They had: 'short tubular dresses, cigarettes in long holders, cloche hats, bobbed hair, plucked eyebrows, bands of diamond bracelets from wrist to elbow, and earrings hanging like fuschias'.

The Eton crop was the fashionable hairstyle of 1925, causing *Punch* to comment in a cartoon caption: 'Grow your hair, man, you look like a girl!' Wide flapping trousers called Oxford bags were introduced for men that year, and for leisure wear shirts with soft collars and brightly-patterned Fair Isle pullovers.

Dresses reached the knee by the mid-twenties.

Britain returns to gold

IN APRIL WINSTON CHURCHILL, Chancellor of the Exchequer in the Conservative Government, announced in his budget speech that Britain was 'going back to gold'.

The Gold Standard was a financial system in which the amount of money in circulation had to be matched by the amount of actual gold – in coins and bullion – in national banks. The rate of exchange between currencies was based on each country's gold reserves. The Gold Standard was suspended in 1914 but before that gold supplies were imported and exported without restriction. Banks guaranteed to exchange paper money for gold. The pledge 'I guarantee to pay the bearer on demand', signed by the Governor of the Bank of England and printed on British bank notes, was backed by actual gold coins.

In 1925 the pound was worth less in exchange for the dollar than it had been in 1914. New York's Wall Street had started to overtake the City of London as the world financial centre. The US was also exporting more of its industrial products and manufactured goods than Britain. Products from Britain's older industries were no longer in great demand. The textile industry suffered and coal, especially, was badly hit by the development of alternative sources of energy and by modernization of the mines in other countries.

Many economists and politicians argued that the only way to restore the economy and enable the pound 'to look the dollar in the face' was a return to the Gold Standard at the old rate of 4.86 dollars to the pound.

Keynesian economics

THE RETURN TO GOLD was opposed by the Cambridge economist John Maynard Keynes. In his book *The Economic Consequences of the Peace*, he had attacked the policy of German reparations. Now in a pamphlet entitled *The Economic Consequences of Mr Churchill*, he warned that a return to gold would be an economic disaster.

The artificial boosting of the pound's value would mean that foreign countries had to pay more for British exports. The Keynesian theory of economics, which sought to modify capitalist society by socialist-type controls, became the basis of government policy in the 1940s.

Cocktail bars

THE COCKTAIL, a new drink from America, was taken up with enthusiasm by the 'smart set' in Britain, and the cocktail bar became the new rendevous for an aperitif. Mixed in a special shaker by a white-jacketed barman, cocktails soon made the pre-dinner sherry seem 'old hat'. Popular ones were:

Manhattan: Two parts of rye whiskey to 1 part of Italian Vermouth, a dash of bitters stirred with cracked ice, strained into glasses, and decorated with a Maraschino cherry.
Sidecar: Equal parts of Cointreau, brandy and lemon juice, shaken with shaved ice and strained into glasses.

A cocktail bar depicted in the French magazine La Vie Parisienne.

Communists jailed

TWELVE LEADING MEMBERS of the British Communist Party, including Harry Pollitt, its general secretary, were sent to prison in October. They were tried under the Incitement to Mutiny Act of 1797 for 'seditious libel'. In articles and speeches they had urged members of the armed services not to use force against strikers if called out in industrial disputes. In a surprise move, the judge offered to release them if they renounced their views. They declined.

The Communist Party of Great Britain was formed in 1920. It frequently applied for affiliation to the Labour Party but was always refused. Though small in numbers it played a vigorous – if ineffective – part in British political life between the wars.

'Jix'

THE MAN MAINLY RESPONSIBLE for the Communists' prosecution was William Joynson-Hicks, the Home Secretary, who was known to all by his nickname 'Jix'. During his time in office – from 1924 to 1929 – he unceasingly hunted out 'Reds under the bed' and was also zealous in a self-imposed crusade against the moral decline he saw everywhere in Britain. A teetotaller and a dedicated church-goer, he was not popular with the Bright Young Things, whose night clubs he called 'the social sewers of London'.

Border problem shelved

BY 1925 THE IRISH BOUNDARY Commission had still come to no firm decision and in December it reluctantly agreed to leave the border as it was. This decision was disliked by hardliners in both North and South. A Council of Ireland, set up to work towards bringing the Irish Free State and Northern Ireland together, was also abandoned. So the stage was set for further decades of 'Troubles' over Ulster.

Hitler publishes *Mein Kampf*

The first volume of Adolf Hitler's autobiography *Mein Kampf* ('My Struggle'), which he wrote in prison after the Munich Putsch, was published in July. A second volume came out in 1926. It did not sell widely in Germany until it was brought out in a 'People's Edition' in 1930. Abroad it was virtually ignored.

The style of the book is long winded and bombastic. In it Hitler expressed his belief in the superiority of the German race and his plans for his country's resurgence. These included solving what he called 'the Jewish problem' and resulted ten years later in his policy of exterminating the Jews in Germany.

In heedlessly ignoring the question of the preservation of the racial foundations of our nation, the old Reich disregarded the sole right which gives life in this world. People who bastardize themselves, or let themselves be bastardized, sin against the will of eternal Providence . . . . Every defeat can become the father of a subsequent victory, every lost war the cause of later resurgence . . . – as long as the blood is preserved pure . . . .
Mein Kampf, translated by D.C. Watt.

Hitler (extreme left) in Tyrolean dress, photographed with Rudolph Hess (second right) and other Putsch leaders, in prison surroundings which look more like those of a holiday hotel. It was in jail that Hitler wrote Mein Kampf.

Sport and the Arts

Impossible quest

THE GREAT GATSBY, F. Scott Fitzgerald's novel published in 1925, seemed to many like a benchmark for the age it depicted. The high-living, fast-spending Jay Gatsby, who was nevertheless broken in the chase after an impossible ideal, seemed to personify the wider quest by many Americans for what has been called 'The American Dream' – a vision of material well-being and spiritual fulfilment which is never quite realized. Fitzgerald's own life and that of his wife Zelda embodied a similar search. He wrote five successful novels, including his first, *This Side of Paradise*, which was a best-seller in 1920. But Fitzgerald died in 1940 with the feeling that he had wasted his talents.

Louis Armstrong (extreme left) playing the trumpet with King Oliver's band.

Jazz age

JAZZ, BORN IN THE DEEP SOUTH of America, moved from New Orleans to Chicago in the twenties and white musicians, such as Bix Beiderbecke and Pee Wee Russell, joined the black 'greats'.

The 'Jazz Age' reached a high spot in 1925 when trumpet player Louis Armstrong launched his band The Hot Fives, which later became The Hot Sevens. Universally known as 'Satchmo' ('satchel-mouth'), he left New Orleans to join King Oliver in Chicago in 1922. He was called 'the epitome of jazz' by another great jazz musician, Duke Ellington, who started playing at the Cotton Club in New York during the same period.

It was also a time when the great blues singer, Bessie Smith, was performing, and pianist Jelly Roll Morton was jazzing up the night-spots with his Red Hot Peppers. The New York district of Harlem became the centre of a negro artistic renaissance. Black theatres, newspapers and jazz bands all flourished there in the 1920s.

Art Deco

AN *EXPOSITION INTERNATIONALE DES Arts Decoratifs et Industriels Modernes* in Paris in 1925 gave the name Art Deco to the modern artistic style. Noted for its streamlined geometric forms, it combined artistic elegance with functional design. Everything from painting, sculpture and architecture to fashion and furnishings were influenced by Art Deco.

Oxford Blues

THE BOAT RACE, the annual Putney to Mortlake contest between Oxford and Cambridge rowing 'eights', excited much partisan feeling in the 1920s among people who lived far away from the Thames and who had never been near either university. Girls made dark or light blue 'favours' from twists of wool and boys wore buttons in the right shade of blue for the side they supported. They chanted rhymes like:

Oxford upstairs
Putting on their braces;
Cambridge downstairs
Winning all the races

– or vice versa.

Cambridge supporters had a field day in 1925 when the Oxford boat sank under Hammersmith Bridge and its crew had to abandon the race.

New homes go electric

IN THE MID-TWENTIES many homes were still lit by oil lamps or gas mantles and most people still cooked on a coal-fired range. But homes were gradually becoming more labour-saving. Kitchen cabinets with pull-out work surfaces were introduced in 1925. Council houses on the new estates were built with 'modern conveniences' such as indoor lavatories, bathrooms and up-to-date cookers. Thermostatic controls for gas cookers were introduced in 1923 with the system of 'regulo' numbers that we use today. In 1926, when the new Central Electricity Board was formed, electricity became available to more homes through a National Grid system. By the end of 1929 a fifth of all homes had electricity laid on.

Go-ahead housewives were able to plug in an electric carpet sweeper or try an electric iron. Frigidaire brought out an electric ice box – forerunner of the refrigerator – in 1923, so giving a new word, 'fridge', to the language.

Electricity was the newest modern convenience for home-owners in the 1920s.

THE HOME OF YOUR CHOICE MUST HAVE ELECTRICITY

For the Ideal Home you must have Electricity available. The Ideal way of achieving this is by the New "LECITE" (Regd.) Wiring System, which embodies the exclusive and most up-to-date All Bakelite Accessories. Hundreds of Householders have wisely asked for the "LECITE" (Regd.) System when building a new home or modernising an old one. It is easily installed, neat in appearance and reasonable in cost. Your Electrical Wiring Contractor will be pleased to give particulars and offer suggestions.

Local Sales Depôts:
LIVERPOOL: 24 Preesons Row, Sth Castle St.
MANCHESTER: 19a Brazennose Street

Branches
In the principal Home Towns
and Overseas

Full particulars on Request

THE LIVERPOOL ELECTRIC CABLE COMPANY LIMITED

Linacre Lane,
Bootle,
LIVERPOOL.

'PHONE: Bootle 1660.
'GRAMS: "Concentric," Liverpool.

Wash day

ELECTRIC WASHING MACHINES were slow to come on the market. For years to come most women continued to do their weekly wash in the old-fashioned way. Winifred Foley, daughter of a miner in the Forest of Dean, remembers:

Our mams . . . lugged the water from the well every day, but the washing was still done regularly every week. When they got the water home, it was heated by a fire under the wash copper, then poured over the dirty washing into a wooden tub; and the clothes and our mams were brought to a lather by the use of the unwieldy heavy wooden 'Dolly' . . . if the weather was wet it must somehow be dried round the fire . . . . Pit clothes took a lot of drying . . . . When there were two or three men in a household working, the family were lucky to see the fire.
Winifred Foley, *A Child in the Forest*

Long-wave transmitter

THE BBC OPENED ITS FIRST LONG-WAVE wireless transmitter at Daventry in 1925. Powered by 25 kilowatts, it was the biggest transmitter in the world and the first-ever long-wave one. It brought 85 per cent of Britain within the reach of radio and enabled many listeners to have a choice of two programmes. Previously they had had to listen to programmes broadcast from their own local stations. There were eight main ones in Britain but reception varied greatly. One man described broadcasts heard in Sheffield as sounding 'like an insurrection in hell'.

Licences

The number of wireless licences issued grew every year and by 1925 had reached over 1½ million.

1926 General strike

Nine-day stoppage – 3 million down tools

FOR NINE DAYS IN MAY Britain was on strike. The miners who were in dispute with the pit owners over hours and wages were joined by over three million workers from other unions – railwaymen, bus drivers, dockers, steelworkers, printers – in what was the country's first, and only, General Strike.

The government called on civilian volunteers to help the Army and police keep emergency services going and to distribute essential supplies such as food and medicines. It was a time of strange contrasts, unusual sights. There were few buses on the roads, no newspapers on sale. Soldiers guarded public buildings and there were even warships at the major ports. In London thousands of office workers walked to work from the suburbs – covering often 15 or 20 miles a day. The early morning milk trains were often the only railway services still running. Hyde Park became a vast milk depot.

Sidney and I travel up by the milk train to London – it is crowded but not a single remark did we hear about the strike . . . the same silence is in the streets, more like a Sunday with the shops open, but with no one shopping . . . here and there officers in khaki, even one or two armoured cars in attendance on strings of motor buses piled up with food . . . .
Beatrice Webb, the Fabian social reformer, in her *Diary*, Vol. IV

Soldiers accompany a convoy of meat lorries during the General Strike.

Strike activity

FOR THE STRIKERS IT WAS A TIME of intense activity. Every area had its own strike committee which published daily bulletins, organized pickets and permits for distribution of supplies, handed out benefits and helped those in distress. They maintained a network of communications with other regions, mostly by the use of motor cyclists.

Thursday, May 6, 1926. Permission granted for bus to travel from Greenbank Hospital to Cockfield with patient . . . . Bishop Auckland holding mass picket tonight . . . two rulley loads of troops arrived in the Market Place . . . . Bank Top Station picket reported that taxi with five men and local grocer arrived with blankets. Request for more pickets . . . .
Darlington Strike Committee log book quoted in *The Long Hard Road* by Wilson Cornforth

Volunteers run transport

FOR UPPER-CLASS university students, Bright Young Things and elderly railway 'buffs', the strike was an exciting opportunity to have a go at running a railway or driving a bus – though most found it harder than they had anticipated. Writer Spike Hughes, then a Cambridge undergraduate, was among them.

To begin with I reported at six o'clock every morning dressed in a blazer and plus-fours and worked as a porter . . . . I did not greatly relish moving boxes of ageing fish, so I ceased to be a porter after a day or so and became a guard . . . . Our train . . . was driven by an engine-driver and a stoker who were rowing Blues. During our maiden voyage our stoker unwisely stood up on the tender as we went under a bridge; but he came back next day, with his head bandaged . . . .
Spike Hughes, *Opening Bars*

Soup kitchens

LIFE IN A YORKSHIRE PIT AREA during the strike is described by miner Gerard Noel:

We had no strike pay. We managed by sharing everything we had. My father had a horse and cart and we went round the village collecting meat and bones from butchers shops. We set up soup kitchens in the village, taking all the poor children standing around. . . .
The Great Lock-out of 1926

stops Britain

Background to conflict

IN 1926 THE COAL INDUSTRY was old-fashioned and badly managed. There were more than 1400 different companies and few had tried to modernize after the war. The pit owners' answer to their problems was to cut miners' wages and make them work longer hours.

A show-down was avoided in 1925 when Baldwin offered the colliery-owners a subsidy to help them pay the miners' wages. He appointed a Commission, under Sir Herbert Samuel, to study the industry's problems. It advocated a total reorganization of the mines with the amalgamation of the smaller pits in each area. But it said the subsidy should cease and for the time-being the miners would have to accept wage cuts.

Not a penny . . .

A.J. COOK, General Secretary of the Mineworkers' Federation responded with the slogan: 'Not a penny off the pay, not a minute on the day'. This stalemate resulted on 1 May in the pits being closed. During the 'lock-out' the Trades Union Congress and the government tried to negotiate a settlement. Talks broke down on 4 May and the TUC called a general strike.

Nearly all trade unionists backed the strike but, in the hope of new negotiations, the TUC called it off on 12 May. The miners stayed 'out' until November when, defeated and near starvation, they finally returned to work on the colliery owners' terms. Nothing was done to reorganize the industry or improve working conditions.

Newspapers

DURING THE STRIKE the government brought out an official paper, *The British Gazette*, edited by Winston Churchill. In it Baldwin told the country: 'Constitutional Government is being attacked . . . . The General Strike is a challenge to Parliament and is the road to anarchy and ruin.'

The TUC produced *The British Worker*, and stressed that the strike was not the start of a 'red revolution' but an expression of support for the miners in an industrial dispute. Union bulletins urged strikers: 'Remain calm and undaunted. Do not be provoked into disorder.'

Though there were, inevitably, many bitter incidents and violent clashes, the General Strike on the whole was characterized by good humour. Football matches organized between police and strikers have become part of legendary lore.

Two sides of the question. Strike newspapers, the British Gazette *and the* British Worker *on 12 May.*

The Trades Disputes Act, passed in 1927, made future general strikes illegal.

Germany joins League

GERMANY WAS ADMITTED to the League of Nations this year and given a permanent seat on the Council. Vernon Bartlett, who became a Foreign Correspondent for the *News Chronicle*, was then on the League's staff. He recalled:

The greatest day in the League's history, and the one I enjoyed most, was 10 September, 1926, the day when Aristide Briand, the French Foreign Minister, welcomed Gustav Stresemann, his German opposite number, as a new member . . . . I remember Aristide Briand as a small, slender man, with a huge leonine head, a cigarette in the corner of his mouth and one of the finest voices I have ever heard. Stresemann, with his little piggy eyes, his red, fleshy neck and his raucous voice, was as moved, and as moving, as Briand himself . . . . After a thousand years of sporadic wars, the French and the Germans, the Western and Eastern Franks, had made their peace in the presence of representatives from every part of the world. On that day at least, one could believe that possibly the politicians' promises were coming true, that perhaps the First World War had been the last . . . .

I Know What I Like.

SECOND-EXTRA-SECOND

Your Newspaper
With no private axes to grind, no selfish personal interests to serve and no financial strings leading to any other source of power or influence.

Los Angeles Record

CITY EDITION 2 CENTS

Thirty-first Year — LOS ANGELES, MONDAY, AUGUST 23, 1926 — Number 9837

VALENTINO DEAD

HOLLYWOOD MOURNS FILM 'SHEIK'S' DEATH

By JIMMY STARR

RUDOLPH VALENTINO, the screen's greatest lover, died this morning, and Hollywood is silent, having waited all night long to hear the latest report of the famous screen sheik's condition.

This morning, as the news came over the wire, Hollywood bowed its head once more for one of its famous ones.

Five years ago "Rudy" started the national wave of the Argentine tango when he appeared in "The Four Horsemen" for Metro, but he came into real popularity when he appeared as the leading man with Agnes Ayres in "The Sheik."

So fine was his performance in that picture that he automatically became a star in his own right when the film was released.

Rudy's famous role as the sheik started the whole world imitating.

• • •

EVERY youth in the country copied Rudy's Argentine peon trousers which he had worn in "The Four Horsemen." Then in the role of "The Sheik" he made bronze complexions and sleek hair even more popular.

Rudy was born in the Italian village of Castellaneta, on May 6, 1895 (31 years ago). He was christened Rudolpho Alfonso Raffaelo Pierre Filiberte Guglielmi di Valentina d Antonguolla.

Rudy first appeared and received screen credit seven years ago under the direction of James Young. His name at that time was Rudolpho de Valentino.

It was in "Roads to Romance," which Young directed with Earle Williams, for Vitagraph, that Valentino was enlisted to do an Apache dance. So clever were his terpsichorean steps that he was given three days' work at $15 a day.

• • •

THIS $45 was Valentino's Hollywood fortune. Later on he appeared with Universal as a villain in a film starring Carmel Myers. He also won a small role with Clara Kimball Young in "Eyes of Youth."

Each part grew until he was finally selected for the leading male role in "The Four Horsemen," which Rex Ingram was directing for Metro studios.

June Mathis, scenarist, is credited with having first "discovered" the young screen sheik. However, James Young, who directed Rudy for Vitagraph, was the first to go on record as having said Valentino would be a great star some day.

Valentino received not more than $250 per week while making "The Four Horsemen." His estimated salary at the time of his death was between $8000 and $10,00 per week.

After appearing in the Ingram feature, Rudy was engaged to appear opposite Alice Lake in "The Uncharted Sea." This part attracted the attention, as did "The Four Horsemen" role, of Nazimova, who selected him immediately for the part of Armand Duval in her version of "Camille."

thought of Valentino and saw that he was engaged for "The Sheik."

After this Rudy played opposite Dorothy Dalton in "Moran of the Lady Letty" and opposite Gloria Swanson in "Beyond the Rocks."

Then came Fred Niblo's version of "Blood and Sand," which placed Valentino, after a series of mediocre films, back into the limelight once more.

Studio trouble resulted over the small salary he was receiving, and Valentino started suit to break his contract with the Lasky organization.

• • •

AFTER many weeks of discussion, a new company, the Rudolph Valentino Productions was organized by J. B. Williams. Valentino completed "The Young Rajah" for Lasky and then went directly to New York, fighting his case and also making public appearances and fulfilling a dancing engagement in Chicago's largest ballroom.

Upon his return to Hollywood, with most of his accumulated fortune wasted upon lawyers in New York, Rudolph was heartsick and discouraged. His new company, which wanted to produce "Cobra," brought only trouble to Rudy's mind. His affairs at home were in turmoil and Rambova is blamed for part of the friction at the studio, which arose between Valentino and his company.

Valentino's small fortune was now practically gone and he was in dire need of funds, once more as he had been four years before.

After considerable trouble, both with his company and his wife, Rudolph decided to disband his organization and signed with Joseph M. Schenck, head of United Artists corporation, who had offered him a long term contract at a huge figure and a percentage interest in his pictures.

• • •

THE friendship between Valentino and Schenck began when the latter aranged $5000 bail after Valentino had been arrested for bigamy and was lodged in the county jail.

It was this move of Schenck's, who had never met the screen idol, personally, which gave Valentino implicit faith in the producer.

Valentino's first picture under the Schenck management was "The Eagle," directed by Clarence Brown and marked a decided departure from any of his other productions.

It was hailed for bringing back a new Rudolph. Then came the sequel to "The Sheik," entitled "Son of the Sheik," for the opening of which Rudolph went to New York when an operation became necessary.

New York meant much to Rudolph, who had once been an apprentice landscape gardener in Central park. This was long before Rudolph had talked himself into a short vaudeville engagement with Bonnie Glass, and it was this act which drew the attention of Joan Sawyer, one of Broadway's famous dancers, who asked Rudolph to form a danc-

LAST ROLE PLAYED

RUDOLPH VALENTINO

• • •

Here's 'Official' Life of 'Sheik'

Here's the official biography of Rudolph Valentino as kept in the files of United Artists' Corporation:

RUDOLPH Alfonzo Raffaelo Pierre Filibert Guglielmi di Valentina d'Antonguolla was born in the little village of Castellaneta, Italy, May 6, 1895. His mother was the daughter of a learned Parisian doctor, Pierre Filibert Barbin. His father, Giovanni Guglielmi, was in his youth a captain of Italian cavalry and later a veterinary doctor.

When Valentino was 11, his father died. He was sent to Dante Alighieri college, where he finished the course at 13. Then he went to a military college where he is said to have been more interested in romantic novels than in studies. It is recorded he was once sent home because he broke out of a room in which he was confined for discipline in order to see the king, a visitor to the school.

gone, he had to seek a job and his first position was as superintendent of the Long Island estate of Cornelius Bliss, Jr.

His next position was as an apprentice landscape gardner in Central Park, New York. At the Civil Service bureau, he was told he was ineligible for a regular position there.

Quite penniless and literally homeless, this phase of the future star's dramatic career was best summarized by the statement that he took any little odd jobs he could get,—shining brass on cars, sweeping out, what not.

Finally the head waiter at Maxim's employed him as a dancer, and so his professional career began. As dancing partner to Bonnie Glass and later with Joan Sawyer, he attained

Last Conscious Word Uttered at 3 O'clock

BULLETIN

By United Press.

NEW YORK, Aug. 23.–Rudolph Valentino, who came to this country as an emigrant and rose to the heights of fame as an actor, died at the Polyclinic hospital here today.

Humbly born, the son of a farmer in Italy, he died with four skilled physicians at his bedside and with the country waiting each word from his sick room almost as it waits for a word from the sick room of a president.

Death came at 12:10 P. M.

Dr. Harold Meeker, one of the attending physicians who was with the actor throughout the night and morning, said he believed the last conscious words were spoken at 3:30 a. m.

At that time, Valentino, still thinking he was to recover from an operation for appendicitis and gastric ulcers, spoke of the days he would spend in recuperation and asked the doctor about trout fishing.

"Do you have plenty of rods and hooks?" the actor asked Dr. Meeker.

At 4 a. m. Valentino became irrational and talked mostly in Italian.

Two hours later he was semi-conscious and lapsed into a coma at 8. From then on he occasionally opened his eyes when his name was called. He died without pain. The cause of death, in medical parlance was "septic pneumonia and septic endocarditis."

Scientists considered a blood transfusion and Edward Day, engineer at the hospital, volunteered a pint of his blood. It was decided, however, that the actor was too weakened to stand the extra strain on his heart.

The corps of physicians then ordered an X-ray. It was found that the pleurisy, which brought about a relapse Saturday when Valentino seemed on the road to recovery, had been followed by septoendocarditis (poisoning of the wall of the heart).

The last official bulletin was issued shortly before noon, when it was admitted that the actor was "rapidly failing."

His temperature had mounted to 105. His pulse was hammering at the rate of 140 strokes to the minute. His respiration was 30 to the minute.

In a few moments the actor was dead.

The operation was performed a week ago Sunday. Valentino had been in New York in connection with the release of one of his pictures, "The Son of the Sheik." He had attended several parties and was in a gay mood most of the week preceding his illness.

After he had been stricken by acute appendicitis he was taken to the hospital.

The ulcerous condition was said to be more of a menace to his health than the appendicitis.

At first it was believed the operation had been completely successful. On Tuesday it was known that periton-

by Drs. Paul E. Durham, G. Randolph Manning and Howard D. Meeker.

The relapse came Saturday. Valentino still showed a remarkable constitution and physicians took hope from his courage. However, the disease traveled slowly but certainly toward the heart and death could not be denied.

After news of his death came today, the telephone girls were immediately beseiged once more.

By Thursday of last week Valentino was in better spirits and hopes were high that his recovery would be complete. He even consented to an interview, through George Ullman, his personal manager.

Valentino had lost consciousness shortly before the end.

• • •

Pola Faints at News of Death

Unconscious and hysterical by turns, crying out her grief over the death of Rudolph Valentino, Pola Negri, reported fiancee of the dead film star, was under the care of two physicians in her Ambassador hotel bungalow today.

The Polish film star's grief was touching.

Informed of Valentino's death by newspapermen, Miss Negri fainted.

Frantically her maid, crying out for aid, summoned th hotel house physician. A few moments later the star's pr vate doctor arrived. Restoratives returning her to conscious ness, Miss Negri wept bitterly. The star was completel unnerved. A few moments later and her grief turned to hysteria.

In her dialect of mixed English and Polish, Miss Negri screamed again and again the name of Valentino.

Again physicians quieted her.

As news reached the studio where she had been working night and day on her new picture, "Hotel Imperial," in an effort to finish her work in order that she might rush to her lover's bedside, officials dispatched messengers, hoping to be able to reach the actress before she had heard the story from other sources.

They were too late.

Mr. and Mrs. Charles Eyton, close personal friends of the star, were the only ones admitted to her hotel bungalow.

Mrs. Eyton remained with Miss Negri, seeking to comfort her.

The star's hysterical condition prevented her from issuing any statement. It could not be learned if she plans to go to New York, should the funerel be held there.

All work on Miss Negri's picture was abandoned.

At her bungalow home none could say whether the star will rush to New York or not.

At the Famous Players studio flags were lowered to

Locarno Treaties

GERMANY'S MEMBERSHIP followed the Locarno Treaties signed the previous December. They settled the boundaries between France and Germany, and Belgium and Germany. Britain and France agreed to evacuate the Rhineland, which their military forces had occupied since the war.

New Middle East Republic

THE LEBANON WAS PROCLAIMED a republic in May with a new constitution providing for a President and a two-chamber Parliament. In an attempt to settle divisions between Muslim and Christian factions, parliamentary seats and Cabinet places were distributed on a religious basis. It was laid down that the President should be a Christian and the Prime Minister a Muslim.

With Syria, the Lebanon had been governed by France as a League of Nations mandate and the new constitution was drafted in Paris. Both countries were promised early independence but Syria did not become self-governing until 1930.

Death of Valentino

THE DEATH OF ROMANTIC SCREEN LOVER Rudolph Valentino, star of *The Sheik* and *The Four Horsemen of the Apocalypse*, caused mass-hysteria in August. He died after an appendix operation, aged only 31. Thousands of wailing film fans queued to view his body, which lay in state in New York's Broadway. So many wanted to attend his funeral that it caused a riot.

The sudden death of Rudolph Valentino was front-page news.

Turkish modernization

CIVIL MARRIAGE AND DIVORCE were made legal in Turkey in September and polygamy was abolished. These were part of a series of reforms aimed at the emancipation of women, who later gained the right to vote and to stand as candidates at elections. They were encouraged to wear Western dress by Mustapha Kemal, who also developed health services, extended education, introduced the Latin alphabet and started a scheme of social security benefits.

Disappearance

AGATHA CHRISTIE, the detective-story writer, disappeared in December and, after a nation-wide hunt by press reporters, was discovered in a Harrogate hotel. No satisfactory explanation was ever given for her 'lost days'. Her book *The Murder of Roger Ackroyd* was published shortly afterwards and became a best-seller – the first of many. Another prolific author of the period was thriller-writer Edgar Wallace. A former journalist, he published 170 novels altogether.

De Valera founds new party

IN IRELAND, DE VALERA SPLIT WITH Sinn Fein and founded a new party, which he called Fianna Fail (Warriors of Ireland). Most of the moderate Sinn Feiners joined it. The IRA had withdrawn its support from De Valera the previous year and set up its own Army Council to direct activities.

The time of the 'Troubles' was vividly re-enacted in the plays of Sean O'Casey. They were staged at the Abbey Theatre, founded in Dublin by the Irish poet W.B. Yeats. Set in the Dublin slums, *Juno and the Paycock* and *Shadow of a Gunman* were produced in 1925 and *The Plough and the Stars* in 1926.

Birth of a future queen

THIS ANNOUNCEMENT was made from 17 Bruton Street, W1, on 21 April: 'Her Royal Highness the Duchess of York was safely delivered of a daughter at 20 minutes to 3 o'clock yesterday morning.'

Sales war

TOBACCO MANUFACTURERS competed in a 'sales war', as ferocious as that of the newspapers in which they advertised their cigarettes. The new feminine market was canvassed and 'brand loyalty' was promoted by the inclusion of cigarette cards. These were first issued in the 1890s, but discontinued during the war. They reappeared in the twenties. Soon there was a new 'fag card' craze, with children avidly collecting sets of pictures of such diverse subjects as wild flowers and cricketers, racehorses and characters from Dickens.

"Craven "A" for Christmas! that's my motto, I know the boys like them"

CRAVEN "A"

These three delightful packings of 150 cigarettes for 7/6, 100 for 5/-, and 50 for 2/6 will provide for most of your Xmas Gifts

Craven "A" Cork-Tipped Virginia Cigarettes are Made Specially to Prevent Sore Throats
MADE BY CARRERAS LTD. 141 YEARS' REPUTATION FOR QUALITY.

In this advertisement the woman's view is used to promote cigarettes which, it is claimed, 'prevent sore throats'. Another tobacco company appealed to women: 'Don't spoil your figure by eating between meals. . . When tempted smoke a Kensitas instead.'

Sport and the Arts

England regain the Ashes

IN AUGUST ENGLAND WON THE ASHES – cricket's most famous trophy – for the first time since 1912. The score stood at two matches all when the final match of the Test series against Australia started at the Oval in London. So great was the excitement when England won by 289 runs that the crowd surged over the pitch, a sight not often seen at cricket grounds in those days.

Heroes of the game were Surrey batsman Jack Hobbs and Herbert Sutcliffe of Yorkshire. In their opening stand in the second innings, Hobbs scored 100 runs and Sutcliffe 161. Hobbs, who was knighted in 1953, played for Surrey from 1905 to 1934 and was the leading batsman of the twenties. During his career he made 197 centuries and his aggregate score of 61,237 runs is still a record.

England's cricketing victory caused wild scenes at the Oval Test Match.

Going to the dogs

GREYHOUND RACING WAS INTRODUCED to Britain from America in 1926 and rapidly became a popular sport. The first track, on which dogs chased a mechanical hare instead of hunting a live one as they did in coursing, was opened at Belle Vue, Manchester, in July. The following year tracks were opened in Edinburgh and at White City, Wembley and Haringey in London. By the time the National Greyhound Racing Club was formed in 1928 there were more than fifty race-courses in Britain. 'The dogs' was also a popular pastime in Ireland and Australia. The most famous greyhound of the period was Mick the Miller who won the Greyhound Derby twice, in 1929 and 1930.

DAILY SKETCH

No. 5,417. LONDON, THURSDAY, AUGUST 19, 1926. ONE PENNY

HOW THE KITCHENER FAKE BEGAN

CROWD'S WILD RUSH AFTER TEST MATCH VICTORY

How the excited crowd at the Oval yesterday rushed across the ground to cheer the English eleven on their great victory over the Australians in the final Test Match. Unprecedented scenes of enthusiasm were witnessed, the crowd for a long time clamouring for speeches from favourite players.

Tubby Teddy

A.A. MILNE'S BOOK *WINNIE THE POOH*, relating the adventures of the tubby teddy-bear belonging to his son Christopher Robin, was published in October. The bear had appeared two years earlier as 'Our Teddy Bear', in a book of verse called *When We Were Very Young*. But now, wrote Milne, 'when Edward Bear said he would like an exciting name all to himself, Christopher Robin said at once, without stopping to think, that he was Winnie-the-Pooh. And he was.'

Another book of verse, *Now We are Six*, came out in 1927. A second book of stories about Pooh, Piglet and their friends was published in 1928 and called *The House at Pooh Corner*. They soon became children's classics.

Pioneering flight

PIONEERING AIRMAN ALAN COBHAM completed a 28,000 round trip from London to Australia and back by seaplane. On his return he landed his plane on the Thames in front of the Houses of Parliament – to 'wake people up' to the possibilities of commercial air services. He said:

The trip has proved that a girdle may be thrown round the world by means of air routes . . . . Soon it may be possible to travel to Australia by a series of aerial stages with bases and connections at certain places . . . . One thing is certain – aviation will be the making of Australia. Vast spaces hitherto meaning days and weeks of travel will be conquered in a few hours by aeroplane.

The Daily Mirror, 2 October

BBC becomes Corporation

IN DECEMBER A ROYAL CHARTER made the BBC into a public Corporation to be run 'in the national interest'. A Board of Governors was appointed and Reith became Director General. When no newspapers were printed during the General Strike, the public had to rely on BBC radio for news. Reith tried to maintain the BBC's independence during the strike but was criticized for refusing to let the Archbishop of Canterbury broadcast an appeal for a return to negotiations.

FINISH OF THE WORLD'S GREATEST FLIGHT

Alan Cobham's plane nearing the Houses of Parliament. This picture appeared on the front page of the Daily Mirror.

Underground extension

As new estates were built in the suburbs and new houses were strung out along the main roads in what was known as 'ribbon development', the London Underground was extended too. It reached Morden in the South in 1926 and passengers could also travel out to Edgware in North London. Buses, now with top decks and pneumatic instead of solid tyres, lengthened their routes too. Long distance 'charabanc' services challenged the railways. Many towns still had trams which ran on rails down the middle of streets, but some had changed to trolley-buses powered by overhead electric wires.

Baird's television

THE FIRST SUCCESSFUL system of television was demonstrated to scientists at the Royal Institution in London by the Scottish scientist John Logie Baird. He had been experimenting with ways of transmitting visual images by radio since the early 1920s. In 1924 he transmitted the silhouette of a Maltese cross for a distance of three yards, with apparatus assembled in his bedroom from a tea chest, a biscuit tin and cardboard discs.

Though struggling against ill-health and in financial difficulties, Baird set up his own Television Development Co. that year. Scientists in America transmitted a picture of President Hoover's face on the screen in 1927, but it was Baird who, in 1928, managed to make the first transatlantic television transmission between London and New York. The first TV broadcast to the public was made by the BBC in 1929.

Nationalist campaign in China

EARLY IN 1927, CHINESE nationalist forces pushed north from their base in Canton in a campaign against the 'war-lords' who had control of most of the country. The army of the Kuomintang captured Nanjing and their commander, General Chiang Kaishek, set up a provisional government there. In April they took Shanghai.

Chiang then decided it was time to drive out the Communists who had been his allies against the 'war-lords'. Thousands of Communists and their supporters were killed in a purge in and around Shanghai and thousands more fled to the south.

The Kuomintang forces pushed on north and took Peking the following year. Meanwhile, the Chinese Communist Party organized themselves into a guerilla force – the Red Army – to fight the nationalists.

Chiang became President of the Chinese Republic but civil war raged intermittently for 22 years until the Communists, under Mao Zedong, finally gained control in 1949.

Chiang Kaishek (centre) during the 1920s.

China

Dr Sun's ideals

THE KUOMINTANG WAS FOUNDED by the Chinese revolutionary leader, Dr Sun Yat-sen, in 1891. He laid down three principles – Nationalism, Democracy and Socialism – which became its basic ideals. Its aims were to rid China of foreign interference and exploitation, develop a modern system of government and create a better life for the millions of downtrodden Chinese peasants.

In 1911 Sun led a revolution which overthrew the old and reactionary Qing [Manchu] Empire. A Chinese Republic was set up but in the hope of uniting various revolutionary factions, Sun allowed the Army commander, General Yuan Shih-kai, to become its first President. When Yuan assumed dictatorial powers Sun and his followers

Communists reorganize forces

MAO ZEDONG, who was then a young librarian, was one of the founder members of the Chinese Communist Party in 1921. In 1923 the party agreed to help the Kuomintang form a nationalist army. When they were driven out four

were driven into exile in Canton. There they set up a rival government. Sun accepted military advice, money and equipment from Soviet Russia and, though he was not a Communist himself, encouraged Communists to join the Kuomintang. When he died in 1925 he was succeeded by Chiang Kaishek, a nationalist with little sympathy for Communist ideals.

years later, they reorganized their forces in the rice-growing, peasant areas of Hunan and Kiangsi where they set up soviets on the Russian pattern. Mao wrote: 'We communists are like the seeds and the people are like the soil. Wherever we go, we must unit with the people, take root and blossom among them.'

In 1930 Chiang started a second campaign against the Communists. They were driven out of Kiangsi and in 1934 undertook what became known as The Long March – a trek of over 2000 miles to set up a new headquarters at Yenan. Though the Communists and the Kuomintang co-operated in fighting the Japanese during the Second World War, the conflict between the two was renewed afterwards.

Peasant life

NEARLY THREE-QUARTERS of the Chinese population were peasants and life for most of them was a hard struggle just to exist. In the areas controlled by them the Communists gave the land which had belonged to the 'war lords' to the people who farmed it. They started a policy of social reforms. Millions of peasants became Communists because they felt that Mao's party was the only one which considered their interests. A peasant member of the Communist Party described his life as a child between the wars:

My family lived near Changchow. I used to cut wood in the mountains, and in the winter I went there to collect bark. I often heard the villagers talk about the Red Army. They said it helped the poor people, and I liked that. Our house was very poor. We were six people. We owned no land. Rent ate more than half our crop, so we never had enough. In the winter we cooked bark for soup and saved our grain for planting in the spring. I was always hungry. One year the Reds came very close to Changchow . . . . They were good to me. They sent me to school for a while, and I had plenty to eat . . . . All the landlords and money lenders and officials were driven out. My family was given land and did not have to pay the tax collectors and landlords any more. Two of my brothers joined the Red Army.
Quoted in Edgar Snow, *Red Star Over China*

Foreign trade

FOR CENTURIES WESTERN POWERS such as Britain and France had used China as a profitable trading base. By various treaties they gained control of important ports, where they kept naval forces and built military garrisons. There were large foreign settlements in all the chief Chinese cities. Both the Kuomintang and the Communists regarded this as foreign exploitation. So, during the nationalist advance the Chinese seized foreign property, threatened foreign citizens and boycotted their trade. In 1927 Britain sent troops to Shanghai to protect British people and property there but, during the 1920s, Western countries were forced to give up most of their bases in China.

American anarchists executed

THE LIBERAL CONSCIENCE of the world was stirred in 1927 by the execution in America of two anarchists – widely believed to be innocent – who had been sentenced to death for murder in 1920. Protest meetings were held in many cities, including New York, Paris and Rome. In London 200,000 people went to a demonstration in Hyde Park.

Nicola Sacco and Bartolomeo Vanzetti, both Italian immigrants, were charged after a payroll robbery in which two men were shot dead at South Braintree, Massachusetts. When arrested they were both carrying guns and Sacco had in his pocket a leaflet about an anarchist meeting at which Vanzetti was to speak.

Many people thought the trial judge was biased. Outside the court he was heard to call them 'anarchistic bastards' and he disregarded strong evidence that they had alibis. Defence lawyers questioned whether they were being tried for murder or for being anarchists.

Seven years of appeals followed. A gangster confessed to the crime. Time after time the executions were postponed. But the judge refused to order a re-trial. Still protesting their innocence, Sacco and Vanzetti died in the electric chair on 23 August, 1927.

I might have lived out my life talking at street-corners to scorning men. I might have died, unmarked, unknown, a failure . . . . Never in our full life could we hope to do such work for tolerance, for justice, for man's understanding of man as we do now by accident. Our words – our lives – our pains – nothing! The taking of our lives – the lives of a good shoe-maker and a poor fish pedlar – all! That last moment belongs to us – that agony is our last triumph!
From the statement issued by Vanzetti from the Death House, Charlestown State Prison, Massachusetts, before the execution.

Fifty years later it was admitted that there had been a miscarriage of justice. Sacco and Vanzetti's names were cleared in 1977 in a special proclamation by the Governor of Massachusetts.

Schooldays in Britain

NEW MOVES IN EDUCATION came in the 1920s. Local authorities were given wider powers after the war and in 1927 the Hadow Report recommended that at 11 children should transfer from a primary to a secondary school and that the school leaving age should go up from 14 to 15. It was not until 1944 that these proposals were put into practice, however. Spending cuts meant that, though the number of secondary schools gradually increased, most children remained at an 'elementary' school for all of their schooldays. Laurie Lee describes 'the lively reek of steaming life: boys' boots, girls' hair, stoves and sweat, blue ink, white chalk . . .' at his village elementary school in the 1920s.

It was a small stone barn divided by a wooden partition into two rooms – the Infants and The Big Ones. There was one dame teacher, and perhaps a young girl assistant. Every child in the valley crowding there remained till he was fourteen years old, then was presented to the working field or factory with nothing in his head more burdensome that a few mnemonics, a jumbled list of wars, and a dreamy image of the world's geography . . . . Through the dead hours of the morning, through the long afternoons, we chanted away at our tables . . . .
Laurie Lee, *Cider With Rosie*

Dancer killed

ISADORA DUNCAN was a dancer whose expressive 'free style' challenged the restrictions of classical ballet. Her tempestuous private life and her flowing garments matched her artistic style. She was strangled when her long scarf caught in the wheel of a Bugatti driven by her lover.

Progressive schools

BOYS PUBLIC SCHOOLS on the traditional pattern, like Eton and Winchester, dominated the private sector in education – but new 'progressive' co-educational schools were being opened in the 1920s as well. Summerhill, which became known as the 'do as you like school', was started by pioneer educationalist A.S. Neill in 1924 and in 1927 the socialist philosopher and mathematician Bertrand Russell, and his wife Dora opened a school called Beacon Hill,

Czech President re-elected

IN MAY, THOMAS MASARYK was re-elected President of Czechoslovakia, the country he had played a major part

where children were given the freedom to develop in their own way. Rather than having to obey rigid rules, they were encouraged to practise self-discipline. Other 'progressive' schools during the period were St Christopher, at Letchworth in Hertfordshire and Bedales in Hampshire.

in forming in 1919 for the Czech and Slovak races who used to belong to the Austro-Hungarian Empire. Masaryk, respected as a statesman of world stature, was President from 1919 to 1935, when he resigned because of poor health. A champion of the small nation-states which had been created by the Treaty of Versailles, he viewed the rise of Hitler in Germany with dismay. He died in 1937, a year before his country was divided up to appease Hitler at the Munich conference.

This class is listening to one of the BBC's new schools broadcasts.

Bradman goes in to bat

DON BRADMAN, the Australian cricketer who was to become the most famous batsman of all time, started his career this season with the New South Wales state team. He scored 118 in his first innings.

Baseball star breaks record

HARD HITTING, HIGH-EARNING baseball player 'Babe' Ruth scored a record 60 home runs in 1927. Baseball fans called him 'The Sultan of Swat'. He joined the New York Yankees in 1920. When their new stadium was built it was christened 'the house that Babe built'.

Composers of the decade

THE FRENCH COMPOSER Maurice Ravel wrote his most successful orchestral piece, *Bolero*, in 1927. Other noted composers of the era were Dmitri Shostakovich, whose First Symphony was performed in Leningrad in 1926, and Igor Stravinsky. Also Russian-born, Stravinsky lived in France during the 1920s and later went to America. His classical masterpiece *Oedipus Rex* was composed in 1927.

Ballet

STRAVINSKY WROTE THE MUSIC for several Diaghilev ballets from *The Firebird* in 1910 to *Les Noces* in 1923. Serge Diaghilev who founded the Ballets Russes and with it a great twentieth-century ballet tradition, died in 1929. The twenties were known as his 'cocktail period'.

Round table set

DOROTHY PARKER, the American short-story writer, was one of the New York wits who belonged to the Algonquin set, a group who met regularly to drink and talk at the Round Table in the Algonquin Hotel. Others included drama critic Alexander Woollcott and Harold Ross, who founded the *New Yorker* magazine in 1925 and edited it for the next 26 years.

The humorist James Thurber joined the staff of the *New Yorker* in 1927 and described Ross as 'at first view, oddly disappointing . . . . Even in a dinner jacket he looked loosely informal, like a carelessly carried umbrella.' Numerous Thurber stories and drawings, including many of the famous Thurber dogs, appeared in the magazine before being published in book form.

Popular tunes

Many homes had pianos in the 1920s. Sheet music of popular songs and dance tunes were snapped up as soon as they came into the shops. The latest hits were also recorded on 78 rpm records made of shellac and played on wind-up gramophones. Young people rolled back the carpet and practised the latest steps to the music of bandleaders such as Jack Payne and Jack Hylton.

A selection of sheet music covers from the twenties.

Solo flight across Atlantic

AN AMERICAN PILOT, CHARLES LINDBERG, became a world hero when he made the first solo non-stop flight across the Atlantic. In a 220 horsepower Ryan monoplane, carrying a heavy load of 451 gallons of petrol and 20 gallons of oil, he left New York on 20 May and landed in Paris 33 hours 39 minutes later.

Paris, May 21 . . . . At 10.24 *The Spirit of St Louis* landed and lines of soldiers, ranks of policemen, and stout steel fences went down before a mad rush as irresistible as the tides of the ocean. 'Well, I made it,' smiled Lindberg . . . . Twenty hands reached for him and lifted him out as if he were a baby. Several thousands in a minute were around the plane. Thousands more broke the barriers of iron rails round the field, cheering wildly. As he was lifted to the ground Lindberg was pale, and with his hair unkempt he looked completely worn out . . . .
New York Times

The talkies arrive

THE SHORT ERA OF THE SILENT MOVIE ended in 1927 when the talkies were introduced. A film with synchronized music had been produced by Warner Brothers in 1926, using a system of sound-on-discs which they called Vitaphone. The first words actually spoken on screen came a year later from Al Jolson in another Warner Brothers' film *The Jazz Singer*. 'Wait a minute,' he declared, 'You ain't heard nothin' yet!'

The first complete all-talking feature film was made by Warner Brothers in 1928. It was called *The Lights of New York*. In the same year they produced another Al Jolson hit, *The Singing Fool*. Audiences cried at his sentimental rendering of the song *Sonny Boy*. Not only the 'talkies' but also the 'weepies' had been born.

Charlie Chaplin was able to follow his 1925 film *The Gold Rush* with another silent movie, *City Lights*, in 1931. Many stars of the silent screen disappeared, however, when talkies arrived because they could not adapt to the new medium.

The Swedish actress Greta Garbo made her Hollywood debut in 1927, in a silent film called *Love*. When she made her first talkie in 1930 the newspaper headlines shrieked: 'Garbo Speaks!'

Household tip

Buy 1oz of saturated solution of permanganate of potash. If when a drop of this is added to a tumbler of water its colour changes to brown, it is unfit to drink. If it remains clear or slightly rose-coloured after an hour it is, broadly speaking, safe. This test should always be applied when sore throats are prevalent, or diphtheria or typhoid is in a house.
Tried Favourites Cookery Book

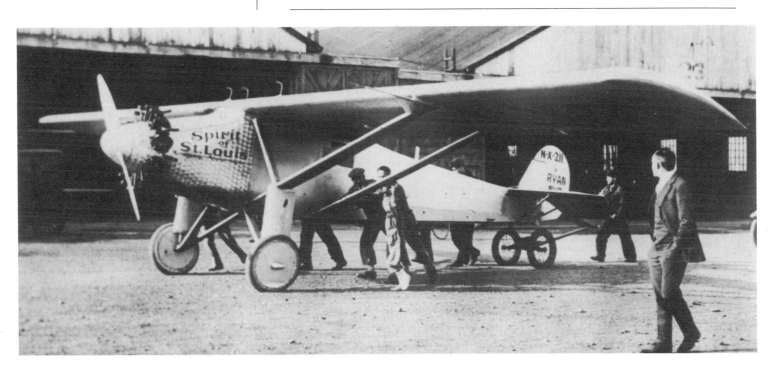

Lindberg's plane, The Spirit of St Louis, *shortly before the epic flight across the Atlantic.*

1928

Five year plan for growth

IN OCTOBER STALIN, now undisputed ruler of the USSR, launched his first Five Year Plan. It laid down targets for the rapid growth of industry and the modernization of agriculture. Stalin believed that this plan was essential if Russia was to survive as a communist country in a hostile world. He feared attack from outside and said in a speech:

Our country is encircled . . . by capitalism. It is impossible to preserve our independence without having an adequately industrialized base for defence.
Quoted in Martin McCauley, *The Stalin File*

The Plan's first aim was to build up heavy industry and increase the production of machinery. Consumer goods, such as clothes and furniture, would have to wait until the country was firmly on its feet. Weekly production targets were laid down for the mines and steelworks and in the factories. There were rewards for success but stiff penalties for failure. Stalin told Russian workers that

The centre of industrialization, the corner-stone, lies in the development of fuel resources, metallurgical production, finally in the development of machinery and tools for production. Either we achieve this or we shall be wiped out.
Quoted in Martin McCauley, *The Stalin File*

Over 1500 new industrial enterprises were built during Stalin's first Five Year Plan. Its success in promoting industrial growth is shown in these figures:

Production in millions of tonnes:	1928	1932
Coal	35.4	64.3
Oil	11.7	21.4
Pig Iron	3.3	6.2
Steel	4.0	5.9

(Quoted in *The Stalin File*)

Collective farms

SIMILAR CHANGES WERE PLANNED for agriculture. Under Lenin the kulaks had become prosperous. In 1927 these peasant farmers refused to sell enough grain to feed the people in the cities and the soldiers of the Red Army because they thought the prices offered by the government were too low.

In a speech Stalin declared:

The only way out of the situation is to overcome the capitalist elements in the village . . . . It is necessary, gradually and resolutely, to re-fashion agriculture on a new technical basis, on the basis of large-scale production, pulling it up to socialist industry.

Small farms were joined together and run as 'collectives' for the benefit of the state. All private farming was abolished. The sale of surplus grain was banned. Stalin spoke of the 'liquidation' of the kulaks. 'Now we are able to conduct a determined offensive against the kulaks, eliminating them as a class', he said.

Slaughter by kulaks

IN RETALIATION THE KULAKS 'eliminated' their livestock, rather than surrender the animals to the collective farm. The Russian writer Mikhail Sholokhov described this in his novel *Virgin Soil Upturned*.

Animals were slaughtered every night. Hardly had dusk fallen than the muffled bleats of sheep, the death squeals of pigs or the lowing of calves could be heard . . . . At dinner-time tables groaned under boiled and roasted meat. At dinner-time everyone had a greasy mouth, everyone hiccoughed as if at a wake. Everyone blinked like an owl, as if drunk from eating.

The feasting did not last long. Peasants who resisted collectivization were either shot, left to starve or sent to forced labour camps. As mechanization increased and tractors replaced horsepower, many other farm workers were directed to work in the factories.

Upturn in farm production

THE EFFECT OF THE PLAN on agriculture was slower than on industry. In the early thirties there was again famine in some parts of the USSR and grain had to be imported. Gradually, however, collectivization did lead to an upturn in agricultural production. The 25 million peasant farms which existed in 1928 were transformed under Stalin into about 100,000 collectives.

Stalin

Stalin ousts Trotsky

Josef Stalin was born to a peasant family in Georgia, South Russia, in 1879 and joined the revolutionary movement as a young man. He became editor of *Pravda* in 1917 and was made Secretary of the Communist Party in 1922. On the death of Lenin his main rival for power was Leon Trotsky, who had been Lenin's Commissar for Foreign Affairs and for War and had also created the Red Army.

While Trotsky urged Communists to strive for world revolution, Stalin agreed by 1924 with Lenin's view that this was impossible in the near future. He declared that 'Socialism in One Country' – Russia – should be the first target. By 1926 Stalin was powerful enough to expel his rivals from the Party.

Trotsky, a Ukranian Jew by birth, had been close to Lenin as a young revolutionary and was favoured by Lenin as his successor. As a practical politician, however, Stalin out-manoevered Trotsky, who was more of an intellectual thinker, and by 1928 was in sole command of the Party.

In 1929 Trotsky was exiled to Turkey. He was killed by a Stalinist agent in Mexico in 1940.

One of Stalin's allies in the early years was Gregori Zinoviev but he, too, was ousted in 1926. Ten years later he was executed for treason, one of the many victims of Stalin's purges in which all who disagreed with his policies were eliminated. Other leading Communists who were expelled were Leo Kamenev (1926), a former ally of Stalin's, and Bukharin (1929).

Josef Stalin took over power in the USSR after Lenin's death.

Peace Pact signed

THE HIGH POINT of the peace movement was reached in 1928 when 65 nations signed a pact renouncing war. Aristide Briand, the French Foreign Minister, suggested an anti-war agreement between France and America in 1927. The American Secretary of State, Frank B. Kellogg, urged that it should be extended to as many countries as possible. As a result, 15 nations signed the Kellogg-Briand Pact at a conference in Paris in August 1928 and 50 more subsequently endorsed it. Major signatories included not only France and the USA but Britain, Germany, Japan and the USSR.

THE AUTOGRAPH HUNTER.

A Punch *cartoon on the Kellogg-Briand Pact shows 'Miss Peace' collecting signatures of peace-keeping nations.*

Floods kill 14 in London

FOURTEEN PEOPLE WERE KILLED when the Thames burst its banks in London during a great storm in January.

The swollen waters of the Thames as they swept through London met an incoming tide of unusual height, with the result that the river overflowed its banks from Greenwich to Kew. Numbers of people were trapped in the basements of dwellings in streets adjoining the river, and no fewer than fourteen were drowned, while great damage was done to property and thousands of people were rendered homeless. Such a flood has not been experienced for 700 years.
Annual Register, 1928.

The Houses of Parliament, Lambeth Palace and St Thomas's Hospital were all flooded and Nine Elms railway goods yard 'resembled a lake'.

In some places the flood was half way up the walls of ground floor rooms . . . groups of poor, agitated people, many with only a single garment hastily flung on over their night attire, stood shivering and bemoaning the fact that their beds were under water . . . .
Daily News, 7 January 1928

Indians boycott British Commission

NATIONALISTS IN INDIA were still pressing hard for independence. In 1928 the British government sent out a commission under Sir John Simon to study the constitutional position. Gandhi's Indian National Congress Party denounced the British for using delaying tactics and decided to boycott the Simon Commission.

At a meeting in December Congress leaders were divided over whether to press for all-out independence or to agree that India should become a British Dominion. Gandhi wanted to keep the link with Britain and persuaded the Congress to demand Dominion status within one year. He declared that if this was not given he would lead a national civil disobedience campaign for Indian independence.

Early in 1929 Britain called a conference on India. Congress leaders would not go because they said they wanted Dominion status, not more talks. A campaign of non co-operation followed in which Indians refused to buy or sell British goods, such as textiles.

'Flapper vote'

IN 1928 BRITAIN AT LAST GOT UNIVERSAL suffrage. The Representation of the People (Equal Franchise) Act gave the vote to all women of 21 and over on the same conditions as men. Called the 'flapper vote', because previously only women over 30 had been able to go to the polls, it added about five million new voters to the electoral register.

America elects new President

HERBERT HOOVER BECAME US President in 1928. He was a Quaker who, after the First World War, went to Europe to direct relief work. Trained as an engineer, he was also a successful businessman when he was appointed US Secretary of Commerce in 1921. He served under two Republican Presidents, Warren Harding (1920-1924) and Calvin Coolidge (1924-1928).

Coolidge's dictum had been 'The business of America is business' and on succeeding him, Hoover pledged to preserve the 'rugged individualism' of the American citizen. Though economic depression loomed on the horizon, he felt that left to itself trade would revive. He looked forward to a time when there would be 'a chicken in every pot and two cars in every garage'.

Clearing up after London's flood disaster.

Lady Chatterley banned

THE LAWS AGAINST 'obscene publications' were rigorously enforced in Britain in the 1920s, especially by 'Jix'. *Lady Chatterley's Lover*, the last major work written by novelist D.H. Lawrence, was printed in Italy in 1928. Copies sent to Britain were seized in the post by police and it was banned because of its explicit sex-scenes and 'obscene language'.

Lawrence, the son of a Nottinghamshire miner, had been regarded as an important literary figure since the publication of *Sons and Lovers* in 1913. In the twenties he also wrote the novels *Women in Love* (1920), *Kangaroo* (1923) and *The Plumed Serpent* (1926). He died in 1930.

Just dropping in

'THIS IS MY FIRST TRIP TO ENGLAND and it is rather funny dropping in by airplane . . . .' – Amelia Earhart, who in June became the first woman to cross the Atlantic by air.

Mickey joins Felix

MICKEY MOUSE WAS BORN IN 1928. Walt Disney's greatest creation started life in a silent cartoon, but took to sound shortly afterwards in *Steamboat Willie* – in which Disney himself dubbed Mickey's voice. Soon Mickey was joined by Minnie Mouse, Donald Duck, Goofy and other characters in *Silly Symphonies*, in which musical pieces were illustrated by animated cartoons.

Disney's characters were preceded in the twenties by other cartoon animals, notably Felix, 'the cat who keeps on walking', and the Bonzo dog. But Disney had that touch of genius that put his characters in a different class. Born in Chicago in 1901, he pioneered colour cartoons and made his first full-length film, *Snow White and the Seven Dwarfs*, in 1934.

"I met a few old friends at Wembley!"

Felix the Cat was usually seen in the cinema but here he features on a postcard.

Bloomsbury Group

THE ASSOCIATION OF WRITERS, artists and intellectuals known as the Bloomsbury Group continued to flourish during the 1920s and it was during this period that its 'arch-priestess', Virginia Woolf, published some of her major works including *Jacob's Room* (1922), *Mrs Dalloway* (1925) and *To the Lighthouse* (1927). A much lighter work, *Orlando*, came out in 1928. Unlike the others, it was an immediate popular success. Virginia Woolf's books were published by the Hogarth Press, run by her and her husband, the political writer Leonard Woolf. In 1928, 16-year-old Richard Kennedy went to work there.

All hands to the pumps with *Orlando*. (We) all lined up at the packing bench and slashed away with our butchers knives in order to send out review copies . . . . Mrs W is a pretty fast worker . . . . *Orlando* is selling like hot cakes. L.W. is terrified we will run out of stock . . . .
Richard Kennedy, *A Boy at the Hogarth Press*

Tipperary Tim's lone finish

THE GRAND NATIONAL RACECOURSE at Aintree was a punishing one for the horses in this period and often, out of 40 or 50 starters, only a handful completed the race. In 1928 all but six of the 42 runners were put out of the race when a horse became lodged on top of the fence at the Canal Turn. At the last jump there were only two left. One fell, and amateur jockey Bill Dutton rode his mount, Tipperary Tim, past the winning post, the only horse to finish. He was a 100-1 outsider.

First antibiotic

THE MOST IMPORTANT SCIENTIFIC discovery of the decade came about by chance. British scientist Alexander Fleming was experimenting on the staphylococcus bacteria, which causes skin diseases such as impetigo. He left the bacteria to develop on some culture plates in his laboratory for a few days in the summer of 1928. When he next looked at them he found that spots of greenish mould had grown on the plates. The mould had killed some of the bacteria.

Fleming discovered that the mould contained an antibiotic, or germ-killing, substance. He called it penicillin. In a scientific paper he wrote:

Penicillin is non-toxic to animals in enormous doses and is non-irritant . . . . It is suggested that it may be an effective antiseptic for application to, or injection into, areas infected with penicillin-sensitive microbes.

The development of penicillin for use in medicine had a dramatic effect on the fight against disease and it was widely used in the Second World War for the treatment of wounded servicemen.

Traffic lights beat jams

THE 1920S SAW A PHENOMENAL INCREASE in road traffic. The number of private cars in Britain went up from 314,000 in 1922 to just over a million by the end of the decade. Lorries and vans, buses, trams and trolley buses brought the total number of motor vehicles up to around 2¼ million.

The volume of traffic caused jams in towns, especially in London. Police on point duty struggled to regulate the flow of vehicles at busy junctions by hand signals until, in 1928, the first traffic lights were introduced.

AN IMPRESSION *by* JOHN CAMPBELL

Woman at the wheel

Does Fashion lead Woman, or Woman lead Fashion? . . . The fashion all women follow is Pratts High Test

Pratts HIGH TEST SEALED

NO DEARER THAN ORDINARY PETROL

PRATTS MOTOR OIL "STOPS THE BEARINGS WEARING"

[*Page seventeen*

Motoring advertisements were often aimed at women drivers during the 1920s.

Women take to the road

MOTORING GAVE WOMEN a new freedom and the 'flappers' took to it in style, especially when the development of the electric self-starter meant that a crank-handle was no longer needed. Car salesmen coined the dictum: 'While men buy cars, women choose them.' They angled their advertisements to appeal to the feminine eye.

Cars became more comfortable during the late twenties and the open tourer was gradually superseded by the closed saloon car. Henry Ford brought out a new Model 'A' in 1927 which, unlike the Model 'T', had refinements like windscreen wipers, and came in a choice of four colours.

Rivalry between the British firms of Austin and Morris brought prices down. The Morris Minor was launched in 1928 at a price of £125. Later it dropped to a straight £100. The first trailer caravan was produced in the 1920s by the Eccles Co. It cost £185.

1929 Wall Street

Fortunes vanish overnight

29 OCTOBER WAS 'BLACK TUESDAY' on the New York Stock Exchange. Millions of shares were sold by panicking investors – and the stock market collapsed with a crash which resounded across the world.

America had been experiencing an artificial boom. Business was flourishing and the price of shares went up and up. Financial speculators made fortunes by clever buying and selling. Thousands of ordinary people 'got in on the act' by borrowing money to buy shares which they hoped to sell later at enough to pay back their debts and still make a profit.

On 24 October the bubble burst. Rumours of dishonest dealings led to a loss of confidence by speculators. Large blocks of shares were suddenly sold and this caused panic among other investors. Soon everyone was rushing to sell – and prices fell dramatically because no one wanted to buy. So many shares – about 13 million – were sold that day that the ticker tape which recorded the prices for the stock-brokers, could not keep up. Many investors found that their fortunes had vanished overnight.

Bankrupt borrowers

Throughout America businesses collapsed and small-time borrowers, unable to pay back the money on which they had hoped to make their fortunes, went bankrupt. Banks closed down and, because people could no longer buy their goods, factories ceased production.

On Wall Street some of the ruined investors took a quick way out by plunging to their deaths from the tops of New York's skyscrapers.

New York, Tuesday. Mr Anthony Snyder, president of the Webster-Eisenlohr Company and of the Union Cigar Company . . . was killed in a fall from a window of his apartment at an hotel. A waiter who served his breakfast said that Mr Snyder lost his balance while looking out of the window. He fell five storeys to instant death.
Daily Mail 30 October 1929

Oh gosh, a friend of mine was making $25,000 a year. They cut him to $5000. He walked right over the Board of Trade Building, the top, and jumped.
Howard Worthington, quoted in Studs Terkel, *Hard Times*

Frenzied scenes in New York

OVER THE NEXT FEW DAYS matters got worse. In spite of reports that the stock market was 'rallying' and attempts by banks to bolster it up with a loan, share prices continued to plunge. Sixteen million shares changed hands for derisively low prices on 29 October and the ticker-tape gave up entirely.

New York, Tuesday. The scenes of feverish mass selling on the days preceding today's climax, spectacular as they were and full of tragedy for unfortunate investors all over the country, were almost trivial by comparison with the struggle in Wall Street today with its attendant slaughter . . . . Today's opening was the wildest in history. Blocks of from 10,000 to 20,000 and 50,000 shares of US Steel, General Motors, General Electric and Canadian Pacific were offered regardless of price, but again there were no takers unless at stupendous concessions.
Daily Telegraph, 30 October

Turbulent scenes in Wall Street after the crash.

crash

Bus companies cash in

CROWDS OF DISTRAUGHT SPECULATORS besieged Wall Street and at one stage the mob was so great that a police riot squad was called out to disperse it. Some businessmen managed to 'cash in' on the disaster, however.

Motor bus companies, hearing that Wall St was on the rampage, quickly arranged a service of specials carrying thousands of visitors to the Stock Exchange and the financial district. Their chief function was to supply colour for news-recording cinema concerns . . . . The buses were labelled: 'Wall Street circus: sanguinary fight between bears and bulls: record slaughter of lambs.' *Daily Telegraph* 29 October

Depression years

THE CRASH WAS FOLLOWED by the Great Depression, which lasted through the thirties. Europe, which since the war had depended on massive American loans, was hard hit when these ceased. Soon there were six million unemployed in Germany alone.

Unemployment rose in America too and there were eight million out of work by 1931. Men who had owned their own businesses had to rely on 'poor relief' payments and 'stand in line' for hand-outs of free food. Before the crash Ben Isaacs ran a clothing business in Chicago –

We lost everything . . . . I couldn't pay the rent. I had a little car, but I couldn't pay no license for it. I left it parked against the court. I sold it for $15 in order to buy some food for the family. I had three little children. . . . I didn't have a nickel in my pocket. Finally people started to talk me into going into the relief. They had open soup kitchens . . . . you had to go two blocks, stand there, around the corner, to get a bowl of soup. Lotta people committed suicide, pushed themselves out of buildings and killed themselves, 'cause they couldn't face the disgrace'.
(Quoted in *Hard Times*.)

STOCK VALUES CRASH IN RECORD STAMPEDE; BANKERS HALT ROUT

CURIOUS JAM WALL STREET TO SEE THE 'SHOW'

Huge Crowd Throngs "Money Lane" Seeking Thrill in Battle of Bulls and Bears

Butcher, Baker and Candlestick Maker Rush to View "World Series" of Finance

From The Inquirer Bureau.
NEW YORK, Oct. 24.—Huge crowds in a holiday mood resembling a confetti of faces from the upper stories of Wall Street skyscrapers surged up and down the narrow streets of the financial district today in search of excitement following rumors that the New York Stock Exchange would close its doors to avert a panic. Brokerage offices were jammed with anxious tape watchers and the floors of the Stock Exchange and Curb were in pandemonium.
Newsboys, clerks, out-of-town visitors, housewives, truck drivers, team-

Stock Slump Fails to Dim Tax Cut Hope

WASHINGTON, Oct. 24 (A. P.).—The view that the recent slumps in the stock market will not affect the administration's tax-reduction programme is held by Treasury officials.

The officials regard the slumps as being more in paper profits than in actual values and believe the action was in the nature of a readjustment of the market and that stock prices generally still were above those paid by people who bought them at ordinary stages some time ago.

BUSINESS OF NATION UNSHAKEN, DECLARE TREASURY OFFICIALS

Officials Assert Underlying Security Not Touched by Slump

Collapse Brings Renewal of Demands That Congress Probe Wall Street

UPSWING ENDS WILD SELLING IN 12,894,650 DAY

N. Y. Exchange Sees Most Violent Drop in Prices Since 1914; Ticker Hours Late

Market Rallies as Morgan and Other Financial Groups Meet and Issue Statement Declaring Trade Sound

From The Inquirer Bureau.
NEW YORK, Oct. 24.—Long withheld buying powers and the reassuring statements of America's most powerful banking interests came to the support of a collapsing stock market today and averted what might otherwise have been the greatest financial debacle in the country's history.
The panic, which threatened to sweep away the billions in values built up during the bull markets of the last several years, was arrested after Wall Street had passed through five hours of trading on its security exchange never before equaled in volume rapidity.

Second Labour government – still a minority

THE LABOUR PARTY won a general election in May and in June Ramsay MacDonald formed Britain's second Labour government. Again it was a minority one. Labour had 287 seats in the House of Commons but the Conservatives, with 261, and the Liberals, who had 59, had a majority between them. Labour had to rely on Liberal support and stick to moderate measures.

The government announced a programme of public works to help the unemployment situation in the distressed areas of the North and in South Wales. But little headway was made. The numbers out of work rose from just over a million in June to nearly two million by the end of the year. The hunger marches of the 30s were foreshadowed by a march to London of unemployed from Glasgow.

Woman's Weekly *instructions to new 'flapper' voters on how to go to the poll.*

The flappers vote

THE 1929 GENERAL ELECTION was the first in which the newly-enfranchised women under 30 were able to vote. Some historians attribute to them the increase of three million in the Labour vote. It seemed fitting, anyway, that 1929 should see the appointment of Britain's first woman Cabinet Minister. She was Margaret Bondfield, a former shop-assistant from Somerset and an active trade unionist, who became a Labour MP in 1923. MacDonald made her Minister of Labour.

854   WOMAN'S WEEKLY

ALL ABOUT THE BALLOT

Now that you've got the vote, don't throw it away through carelessness. Here are some facts about the ballot, and a few simple hints that will keep you right on polling day

IF you are one of the new women voters, you won't have to wait very long after getting the vote for a chance to use it.

It was only on the first of May that the new voting lists came into force, and before May is out you will, if you do your duty as a citizen, be putting a cross on a ballot paper against the name of your chosen candidate.

NEW VOTERS—A NEW ELECTION

IT'S only right that the one thing should come close on the heels of the other. Every time Parliament passes an act that adds a new class of people to those entitled to vote, the existing House of Commons signs its own death warrant. You see, it is one of the unwritten laws of our Constitution that, when this happens, there must be a General Election, because so many new voters having come into existence, the House of Commons no longer represents the electors.

The new voters, as well as the old, must be given a chance of saying what M.P.'s they want.

That is why the General Election is coming along now, instead of waiting till the full five years that can elapse between elections. *It is coming now because of you, and to allow you to use your vote as quickly as possible.*

Perhaps that's an additional reason why you should use your vote—but you probably don't require any additional reason. As you have read these articles you have seen how important the vote is, and why, for your own sake, for the sake of your fellow-women, for the sake of the nation's homes and the nation's children, you must use it, and use it wisely.

THE POLLING BOOTH

SO we'll take it that you have made up your mind that, when the day comes, you will go to the polling-booth.

There, after you have told the official in charge your name and address, and he has checked up the fact that you're on the voter's roll, he will give you a ballot paper.

Let's suppose there are three candidates—Brown, Jones and Robinson. They will appear in that order on the ballot paper, because that is the alphabetical order. And you have to put a cross against the name of the candidate you want to see M.P. for your constituency. Say this candidate is Jones—your ballot paper, after you've marked it, will look like this :

Brown, Albert	
Jones, Henry	X
Robinson, Richard	

These names, of course, are fictitious—they are just examples.

FIND OUT BEFORE YOU GO

THERE'S one point you will notice about the ballot paper—it doesn't tell you anything about the candidates except their names.

It doesn't say, for instance, that Jones has been M.P. for the constituency for thirty years, and has always looked after its interests ; or that Brown is an expert on local government, and has been mayor of the town ; or that Robinson has served his country in the Civil Service, or is well-known as a temperance worker.

These are points which you must find out beforehand—you should make a point of learning what you can about the personalities and the records of all the candidates.

The ballot paper doesn't even say that one of the candidates is a Conservative, another a Liberal, and another a Socialist. You must find that out before you go to the polls.

ONLY MARK THE "X"

AT every election there are a certain number of spoilt ballot papers. These don't count—they are votes thrown away. Don't make any mistake with yours. Remember, the "X" against the name of the chosen candidate is all that you are allowed to put on the paper. Unless you are in one of the few double-member constituencies, you mustn't put two crosses. And you mustn't put any other mark of any kind except the "X." If you write "Good old Jones." on the ballot paper, even if you've put in the "X" in the right place, *your vote won't count !*

You needn't be afraid to vote for the candidate you think will make the best member. The ballot is secret—nobody but yourself will ever know how you vote. And though canvassers may ask you to say whom you are voting for before polling day, and other people may ask you on the day itself, you needn't tell them unless you want to.

THE RESULT

ONCE you have voted, you will naturally be anxious to know if your candidate has been successful. But counting the votes in an election is a long business, and it will be longer than ever this time, because there will be more votes to count. So it may be next day before the result is declared.

Let us hope your candidate will get in. But even if he doesn't, there is no need to despair. He may have better luck next time. In any case, if you have voted for what you believe is the right man and the right party, you have done your duty as an elector.

Apartheid policy in South Africa

IN 1929 PEOPLE IN SOUTH AFRICA started using the Afrikaans word *apartheid* to describe racial segregation. In that year General James Hertzog's Nationalist Party won a decisive election victory over General Smuts' more liberal South African Party. Hertzog, who had been Prime Minister since 1924, saw this as an endorsement of his plans for restricting blacks' and coloureds' voting rights and for purchasing more land for 'native' African reservations.

Pope and State: split ended

A LONG BREACH BETWEEN the Italian State and the Papacy was healed in 1929 when Mussolini signed a Lateran Treaty with the Pope. The Catholic Church had been in opposition to successive Italian governments since 1870, when the newly-unified Italian state challenged Papal power. Though formerly anti-Church, Mussolini paid the Pope compensation for territory seized by the state and established the Vatican City in Rome as an independent papal state. In return he got Catholic support for his Fascist government.

This came into effect that same year when Catholics were told to vote for the Fascist list of general election candidates. Under a new electoral law they had only one other option – to vote against it. The electoral roll had been reduced from ten to three million by the abolition of universal suffrage and voters were offered one list of candidates drawn up by the Fascist Grand Council. They had to accept or reject all the names en bloc.

Valentine Massacre

AL CAPONE'S RULE OVER CHICAGO'S gangland continued throughout the decade. From his headquarters in the Lexington Hotel he ran bootlegging enterprises, protection rackets, gambling clubs, greyhound tracks and betting businesses. Numerous city officials, including the Mayor, were reputed to be 'in his pocket'.

Capone's greatest enemy was rival gangster 'Bugs' Moran. On 14 February seven of Moran's men were waiting to meet their boss at a liquor warehouse. Before he arrived they were mown down by assailants with machine guns. Moran missed the St Valentine's Day Massacre by minutes.

Capone was in Florida at the time but, though the gunmen were dressed in police uniforms, no one doubted that the killings were the work of his gang. Although Capone was responsible for several hundred murders he was never charged with any of them. His reign ended in 1932 when he was sent to prison – for tax evasion.

Gory aftermath of the St Valentine's Day massacre.

Poor Law abolished

THE POOR LAW WAS ABOLISHED IN 1929. Started in the sixteenth century to provide 'parish relief' for the needy, it developed during the nineteenth into a notoriously harsh system under which paupers were sent to toil in workhouses by specially appointed Boards of Guardians. Now, local authorities were given the responsibility for those in need and workhouses were closed or turned into hospitals. Yet for many years elderly people faced with debts still feared that 'we'll all be in the workhouse' and the stigma of 'going on the parish' for public assistance remained.

Palestine problems

SERIOUS ANTI-JEWISH RIOTING BY ARABS took place in Palestine in 1929. The territory had become a British mandate in 1923. The League of Nations agreement incorporated the Balfour Declaration of 1917, under which Britain was to be responsible for Palestine until she was ready for independence. In this Britain promised to support the plan that Palestine should become the Jewish national home. Large numbers of Jewish immigrants arrived in Palestine during the 1920s, but now Britain had to face the problem of the Arabs who also lived there and regarded Palestine as their home. Palestine became the Jewish state of Israel in 1948.

Seagrave smashes speed record

ATTEMPTS TO SET NEW LAND SPEED records caused excitement in the 1920s as the fastest cars edged nearer to the 200 mph barrier. The record was raised to 133.75 mph at Brooklands in 1922. Then, on the straight and level stretch of Pendine Sands in Wales, Malcolm Campbell reached 146.36 in 1924 and 150.87 a year later.

Another British driver, Henry Seagrave, driving a 1000 hp Sunbeam, broke the record with a speed of 203.70 mph at Daytona Beach, Florida in 1927. Two years later he set a new record of 231.44 mph in his streamlined car, the *Golden Arrow*. He was killed the following year during an attempt to break his own water speed record of 98.76 mph.

Surrealist films

SALVADOR DALI, the most famous of the Surrealist painters, moved to Paris from Spain in 1929 and made his first film, *Un Chien andalou*.

Surrealism grew out of the pre-war anti-art movement known as Dadaism which attacked the false values of art and society. In a Surrealist manifesto the French poet, André Breton, explained that the movement wanted to transform human existence by merging the unconscious with reality to produce an ideal *surrealité*. Surrealist painters such as Max Ernst and René Magritte used a realistic style to depict subconscious thoughts. Dali went further than them by trying to present not just an unconscious dream-state but the experiences of delirium and paranoia.

Modern sculptors

SURREALIST PAINTINGS were greeted with outrage by many members of the general public and so were the works of modern sculptors such as Henry Moore and Jacob Epstein.

Epstein's sculpture of *Rima*, naked goddess of the forest, which was erected in Hyde Park, London in 1925, was regularly covered with tar and feathers or painted green. His figures depicting *Night and Day*, sculpted in 1929 for London Transport, were too high up to be tarred – but some protestors threw bottles at them.

Pictures like this one on the cover of Peg's Paper *attracted romantic readers to the popular story magazines.*

Light reading

THE BOYS OWN PAPER celebrated its fiftieth birthday in 1929, still publishing the traditional type of school stories which had been popular before the war. Newer publications included comics for younger children like the colourful *Jungle Jinks*, *Tiger Tim's* and its stable-mate *Playbox* which featured 'Tim's jolly sister', Tiger Tilly.

Newspaper strip cartoons about such characters as Dot and Carrie, Pip, Squeak and Wilfred, or Mutt and Jeff, were scanned by thousands daily, while women's magazines such as *Peg's Paper* were bought for their torrid love stories. Prolific writers were Ruby M. Ayres and Ethel M. Dell. The daring romances of Elinor Glyn were regarded as even more 'hot stuff'. She invented the description 'she's got "It"' meaning sex-appeal. In Hollywood, film star Clara Bow was given the label 'The "It" girl'.

Zeppelin circles world

THROUGHOUT THE DECADE many people thought that the future of air travel lay with the airship rather than the aeroplane. They were further convinced in 1929 when the German airship, Graf Zeppelin, completed a round-the-world trip. In 1928 it had made its first Atlantic crossing and in the same year a regular transatlantic Zeppelin service came into operation.

Happy snaps – in colour

Photographic films in the 1920s were black-and-white, but experiments were being carried out into colour processing and in 1929 Kodak produced its first 16mm colour film.

Colour was not available, however, for the box-camera which was the most widely used camera during a decade when thousands took up the new hobby of amateur photography. With a fixed focus lens and a black-and-white roll film, which could be taken to the local chemist for development, the box-camera was cheap to buy and simple to use. It enabled families throughout the land to stick 'snapshots' of seaside bathing groups and beautiful babies into their family albums.

Mauretania loses Atlantic Prize

UNTIL 1929 CUNARD'S *MAURETANIA* held the 'Blue Riband' for the fastest time across the Atlantic. She first won it in 1907 but after 22 years the prize was wrested from the ageing liner by the German ship *Bremen*, just launched that year.

The *Mauretania* was the sister ship of the ill-fated *Lusitania*, which was sunk by a German submarine in 1915. In the twenties she plied the Atlantic with Cunard's other two great passenger liners, the *Aquitania* and the *Berengaria*. They offered passengers on the four-day crossing to and from New York all the lavish facilities of a luxury floating hotel. Nearly a hundred dishes were listed on the menu for the *Aquitania's* sumptuous first-class dining-room, where a full orchestra played the latest Palm Court hits to diners in evening-dress. The wine list, too, was expensive but passengers were informed that 'due to the motion of the ship' it was not possible to carry vintage bottles.

R.M.S. "FRANCONIA

Some of the great ocean liners of the decade shown on cigarette cards.

R.M.S. "MAURETANIA"

S.S. "DUCHESS OF RICHMOND"

R.M.M.V. "CARNARVON CASTLE"

Time Chart

World News	Sport and the Arts	Science and Technology
1920 (January) prohibition in America. League of Nations holds first session. British National Insurance Act gives unemploy- ment benefit to most workers. (October) Russo-Polish Treaty signed. (November) George V unveils Cenotaph. Black and Tans recruited for Ireland.	Charlie Chaplin produces *The Kid*. *Main Street* by Sinclair Lewis published. Flaherty films *Nanook of the North*. William Tilden becomes Men's Singles tennis champion at Wimbledon – first US win.	First public wireless broadcast – Melba sings. Celanese material on market.
1921 (March) Lenin starts New Economic Policy. Kronstadt mutiny crushed. British miners strike, other unions refuse support. (April) German reparations fixed. (June) George V opens Ulster Parliament. (August) R38 airship disaster. (December) Anglo-Irish Treaty signed setting up Irish Free State.	Jack Dempsey defeats Georges Carpentier in world heavyweight boxing match. Picasso paints *Three Masked Musicians*. *Crome Yellow* by Aldous Huxley and *Women in Love* by D.H. Lawrence published.	Discovery of insulin. Einstein awarded Nobel Prize. Marie Stopes opens first birth control clinic.
1922 (March) Egypt becomes independent. Gandhi imprisoned. (August) Michael Collins killed during Irish civil war. (September) Chanak crisis. (October) Lloyd George resigns. Bonar Law becomes British Prime Minister. Mussolini's March on Rome. (November) Turkish Republic founded. (December) USSR formed.	Johnny Weissmuller swims 100 metres in less than one minute. T.S. Eliot writes *The Waste Land*. *Ulysses* by James Joyce published. Tutankhamen's Tomb discovered.	Austin 7 produced. British Broadcasting Company formed.
1923 (January) French troops occupy Ruhr. (May) Baldwin becomes British Prime Minister. Ceasefire in Ireland. (August) Calvin Coolidge becomes US President on death of Warren Harding. (September) Military coup by de Rivera in Spain. (November) Hitler's Beer Hall Putsch.	First issue of *Radio Times*. Reith becomes Managing Director of BBC. First FA Cup Final at Wembley.	Tetanus and Diphtheria immunization introduced. 'Big Four' railway groups set up.
1924 (January) First Labour government in Britain. Death of Lenin. (April) Dawes plan introduced for German reparations. British Empire Exhibition at Wembley. (June) Murder of Matteotti. (October) Zinoviev letter sent; Labour loses election.	Olympic Games held in Paris. Gershwin composes *Rhapsody in Blue*. *The Green Hat* by Michael Arlen published. Plays performed in London: *The Vortex* by Noel Coward; *St Joan* by George Bernard Shaw.	Imperial Airways formed. Bugatti T35 produced. BBC Schools Broadcasts start.

Time Chart

World News	Sport and the Arts	Science and Technology

1925

The Charleston comes to Europe.
(March) Chiang Kaishek becomes Kuomintang leader.
(April) Britain returns to the Gold Standard.
(July) Hitler's *Mein Kampf* published.
(October) British communists jailed.
(December) Locarno Treaties.
Irish Boundary Commission wound up.

Art Deco exhibition in Paris.
Films: Chaplin's *Gold Rush*; Eisenstein's *Battleship Potemkin*.
Louis Armstrong forms the Hot Fives.
The Great Gatsby by F. Scott Fitzgerald published.
Steve Donoghue wins the Derby for the sixth time.

BBC opens long-wave transmitter at Daventry.
Wireless licences exceed 1½ million.

1926

(April) Princess Elizabeth born.
(May) British General Strike.
Lebanon becomes a republic.
(August) Death of Rudolph Valentino.
(September) Germany admitted to League of Nations.
Reforms in Turkey.

England win back the Ashes at cricket.
Greyhound racing introduced to Britain.
Jack Dempsey loses world heavyweight boxing title to Gene Tunney.
BBC becomes a public service Corporation.
A.A. Milne writes *Winnie the Pooh*.
The Plough and the Stars by Sean O'Casey produced in Dublin.

Baird demonstrates TV.
Alan Cobham completes round-trip flight to Australia.
Central Electricity Board formed.
First combine harvester in Britain.

1927

(April) Kuomintang takes Shanghai. Chiang attacks communists.
(May) Masaryk re-elected President of Czechoslovakia.
Trades Disputes Act passed in Britain.
(August) Mao Zedong organizes Red Army in China.
Sacco and Vanzetti executed in America.
(December) Trotsky exiled from USSR.

Helen Wills wins women's singles for first time at Wimbledon.
Babe Ruth hits record baseball score.
Henry Seagrave exceeds 200mph in land speed bid.
To the Lighthouse by Virginia Woolf published.
Ravel composes *Bolero*; and Stravinsky *Oedipus Rex*.

First sound film produced.
Lindberg makes first solo flight across Atlantic.

1928

(January) 14 killed in London floods.
(July) 'Flapper Vote' in Britain..
(August) Kellogg-Briand peace pact signed.
(November) Herbert Hoover becomes US President.
(December) Indian National Congress demands Dominion status for India.

Tipperary Tim finishes alone in Grand National.
D.H. Lawrence's novel *Lady Chatterley's Lover* banned.
Mickey Mouse created.

Penicillin discovered.
Baird makes television transmission between London and New York.
Morris Minor launched.
Traffic lights introduced.

1929

(February) Lateran Treaties in Italy.
St Valentine's Day Massacre in Chicago.
(June) Second Labour government. First woman Cabinet Minister appointed.
(August) Arab-Jewish rioting in Palestine.
(October) Wall Street Crash.
Unemployment rises.

Salvadore Dali makes Surrealist film.
Epstein completes *Night and Day* Sculpture.
Seagrave breaks land speed record in the *Golden Arrow*.

Graf Zeppelin makes round-the-world flight.
Kodak produces first 16 mm colour photographic film.

Key figures of the decade

Louis Armstrong (1900-1971)

As a boy Armstrong was sent to a negro reform school in New Orleans, where he learnt to play the cornet. After changing to the trumpet and moving to Chicago he formed his own band in 1925 and became famous for his gravel-voiced singing. His band toured Europe· in the 1930s and went on a world tour in the 1960s.

Stanley Baldwin (1867-1947)

Baldwin was the son of a prosperous iron-master and became Conservative MP for Bewdley, Worcestershire, in 1908. He became Prime Minister in 1923 and held the post again from 1924-1929, a period which included the General Strike. As Prime Minister from 1935-1937 he had to cope with another crisis – the Abdication of Edward VIII. He retired in 1937 and was created Earl of Bewdley.

Charlie Chaplin (1889-1977)

Born a Londoner, Chaplin went to Hollywood in 1913 and joined Mack Sennett's Keystone Comedies. He soon adopted his famous tramp's outfit with bowler hat and cane. His silent films were a unique blend of slapstick comedy and pathos. It was not until 1940 that he made his first complete sound film, *The Great Dictator*. A left-wing sympathiser, he left America during the anti-Communist investigations of the 1950s to live in Switzerland. He was knighted in 1975.

Chiang Kaishek (1888-1975)

General Chiang Kaishek became Kuomintang leader in 1925 and President of the Chinese Republic in 1928. He led the resistance to the Japanese during the Second World War. When Mao Zedong set up the Chinese People's Republic in 1949 he fled to Formosa and set up a rival Nationalist government there.

Noel Coward (1899-1973)

After *The Vortex* in 1924, Coward achieved many more theatrical successes. His 'hit' plays and musicals included *Bitter Sweet* (1929), *Private Lives* (1930), *Cavalcade* (1931) and *Blithe Spirit* (1941). During the war he made an epic naval film, *In Which We Serve*. He is also remembered for his many witty songs, such as *Mad dogs and Englishmen*.

Eamonn De Valera (1882-1975)

De Valera was born in New York and had a Spanish father and an Irish mother. Educated in Ireland, he took part in the Easter Rising of 1916 and was Sinn Fein leader from 1917-1926. He founded the Fianna Fail party in 1926 and was Prime Minister from 1932-1948, keeping Ireland neutral during the war. He was Prime Minister again from 1951-1954 and from 1957-1959, when he became President of the Irish Republic.

Alexander Fleming (1887-1955)

A farmer's son from Ayrshire, Fleming studied medicine at St Mary's Hospital, Paddington which became the base for most of his future research, including the discovery of penicillin in 1928. In 1945 he shared the Nobel Prize for Medicine with the two scientists who continued research into the antibiotic: Howard Florey and Ernest Chain.

Francis Scott Fitzgerald (1896-1940)

The American writer F. Scott Fitzgerald captured, more than any other, the spirit of the 1920s. His first two novels made him rich and then he and his wife Zelda embarked on a life of extravagance and excessive drinking. Though he published *The Great Gatsby* in 1925, his next novel, *Tender is the Night*, was not completed until 1934. In that year Zelda became a patient in a psychiatric clinic. Fitzgerald was working on his next novel, *The Last Tycoon*, when he died.

Mohandas Karamchand Gandhi (1869-1948)

Trained as a lawyer, Gandhi left Bombay to spend over 20 years fighting racial discrimination in South Africa. On returning to India he led the campaign of civil disobedience against British rule. He was imprisoned many times but later co-operated in producing plans for Indian independence in 1947. He was assassinated by a fanatic in 1948.

Key figures of the decade

George Gershwin (1898-1937)

Gershwin started work as a pianist in a New York music shop, playing popular tunes to sheet-music customers. At the age of 19 he wrote his own song, *Swanee*, which sold over a million copies. *Rhapsody in Blue* (1924) was followed by other successes including the jazz opera *Porgy and Bess* (1935).

Paul Klee (1879-1940)

Born near Berne in Switzerland, Klee studied art in Munich and taught at the Bauhaus in Germany from 1920-1933. He returned to Berne in 1934 because of Nazi oppression. He was a leading abstract painter and notable works include *A Girl's Adventure* (1922) and *Uncomposed Objects in Space* (1929).

Suzanne Lenglen (1899-1938)

The French tennis star won the Wimbledon Women's Singles title six times but in 1926 walked out of the championships following a reprimand from the referee when she was late for a match. She never played there again. She opened a tennis school in Paris but died from pernicious anaemia at the age of 39.

James Ramsay MacDonald (1866-1937)

Brought up in poverty in the Scottish fishing village of Lossiemouth, MacDonald became the first secretary of the Labour Representation Committee in 1900. He was elected as a Labour MP in 1906 and in 1924 became Prime Minister of the first Labour government. He headed a Labour government again in 1929 but in 1931 formed a National coalition government with the Conservatives. For this he was branded 'traitor' by most of his party. He resigned in 1935.

Benito Mussolini (1883-1945)

Born in Northern Italy, the son of a blacksmith, Mussolini became a journalist and socialist agitator, but broke with the Socialist Party in 1915 because it opposed the war. He became a Fascist and in 1922 was appointed Prime Minister of a Fascist government, assuming dictatorial powers in 1928. Under him, Italy invaded Abyssinia (Ethiopia) in 1935 and annexed Albania in 1939. Italy entered the war on Germany's side in 1940, but after a series of military defeats Mussolini was forced to resign in 1943. He was captured and shot by Italian anti-Fascists in 1945.

Josef Visarionovitch Stalin (1879-1953)

Stalin was the son of a cobbler from Georgia, South Russia. He joined the revolutionary movement as a young man and was made secretary of the Communist Party in 1922. By 1928 he had complete power in the USSR. During the 1930s he conducted rigorous purges to eliminate his opponents. In 1940 he took Russia into the Second World War on the side of the Allies and was regarded as a heroic war leader. After his death there was a revulsion in Russia against his brutal policies at home and in 1961 his embalmed body was removed from its place of honour in Red Square.

Marie Stopes (1880-1958)

Marie Stopes was born in Edinburgh and began her career as a botanist, becoming the first woman to gain a doctorate at the Botanical Institute in Munich. After an unhappy first marriage and divorce, she decided to campaign against ignorance in sexual matters and became a pioneer of birth control methods. She opened her first birth control clinic in London in 1921, trained nurses to work in further clinics, lectured and wrote books on the subject.

Books for further reading

Books about the 1920s:
Michael Anglo, *Nostalgia. Spotlight on the 1920s*, Jupiter Books, 1976
Robert Graves and Alan Hodge, *The Long Weekend, A Social History of Great Britain 1918-1939*, Hutchinson (paperback edition), 1985
Carolyn Hall (ed.), *The Twenties in Vogue*, Octopus, 1983
Monica Hodgson, *Life in Britain in the 1920s*, Batsford, 1987
Alan Jenkins, *The Twenties*, Heinemann, 1974
Graham Mitchell, *The Roaring Twenties*, Batsford, 1986
R.J. Unstead, *The Twenties*, Macdonald, 1982

Autobiographies by people who grew up in the 1920s:
Winifred Foley, *A Child in the Forest*, Futura, 1974.
Richard Kennedy, *A Boy at the Hogarth Press*, Penguin, 1972
Laurie Lee, *Cider with Rosie*, Penguin, 1981
Ethel Mannin, *Young in the Twenties*, Hutchinson
Jean Metcalfe, *Sunnylea, A 1920s Childhood Remembered*, Michael Joseph, 1980
Mary Wade, *To the Miner Born*, Oriel Press, 1984

General histories:
B.W. Beacroft and M.A. Smale, *The Making of America*, Longman, 1982
Susan Briggs, *Those Radio Times*, Weidenfeld and Nicolson, 1981
Hugh Brogan, *A History of the United States of America*, Longman, 1985
Penelope Byrde, *A Visual History of Costume: The Twentieth Century*, Batsford, 1986
Taylor Downing (ed.), *The Troubles*, Thames Television/Macdonald/Futura, 1980
B.J. Elliott, *Hitler and Germany*, Longman, 1966
Harold Evans, *Front Page History*, Quiller Press, 1984
S.R. Gibbons and P. Morlcan, *The League of Nations and UNO*, Longman, 1970
Sarah Harris, *The General Strike*, Dryad Press, 1985
C.A.R. Hills, *The Hitler File*, Batsford, 1980
F.S.L. Lyons, *Ireland Since the Famine*, Weidenfeld and Nicolson, 1971
Martin McCauley, *The Stalin File*, Batsford, 1979
Peter Moss, *Modern World History*, Hart-Davis, 1978

John Robottom, *Modern China*, and *Modern Rossia*, both in Longman's Modern Times series
A.J.P. Taylor, *The Origins of the Second World War*, Penguin, 1964
Studs Terkel, *Hard Times*, Allen Lane, Penguin Press, 1970
Sydney Wood, *Britain's Inter-War Years*, Blackie, 1975

Some novels written in or about the 1920s: (all available in paperback).
Michael Arlen, *The Green Hat*.
Agatha Christie, *The Murder of Roger Ackroyd*.
F. Scott Fitzgerald, *The Beautiful and Damned, The Great Gatsby, Tender is the Night*.
Dashiell Hammett, *The Maltese Falcon*.
Ernest Hemingway, *The Sun Also Rises, A Farewell to Arms*.
Aldous Huxley, *Crome Yellow, Antic Hay, Point Counter Point*.
D.H. Lawrence, *Women in Love, Lady Chatterley's Lover*.
Sinclair Lewis, *Main Street, Babbitt, Elmer Gantry*.
Mikhail Sholokhov, *Virgin Soil Upturned*.
Evelyn Waugh, *Decline and Fall, Vile Bodies, Brideshead Revisited*.
Virginia Woolf, *Mrs Dalloway, To the Lighthouse*.

Acknowledgments

The Author and Publishers would like to thank the following for permission to reproduce illustrations: BBC Hulton Picture Library for the front and back covers, the frontispiece, and pages 4, 6, 7, 9, 13, 15, 18, 20, 24, 25, 26, 34, 36, 40, 48, 50, 53, 55, 60 and 63; Dover Pictorial Archive for page 38; John Frost Historical Newspaper Service for the front cover and pages 10, 30, 43, 44, 46, 47, 61, 62, 64; the Grange Museum, Brent for pages 32 and 58; the Pat Hodgson Library for pages 8, 12, 21, 27, 33, 45, and 57; the London Transport Museum for the front cover; the National Museum of Labour History for page 14; Peter Newark's Western Americana and Historical Pictures for the front cover; the Newcastle Chronicle and Journal Ltd for page 42; Punch Publications Ltd for pages 31 and 56; Marie Stopes House for pages 4 and 17; the Weimar Archive for page 25; the Wimbledon Lawn Tennis Museum for the front cover. The illustrations on pages 5, 23, 28, 29, 35, 37, 39 and 51 are from the Publishers' archive and those on pages 16, 22, 41, 52, 59 and 65 are from the Author's collection. Crown copyright material in the Public Record Office is reproduced by permission of the Controller of Her Majesty's Stationery Office.

Index

Numbers in **bold** type also refer to illustrations